Roella —
Reach for the stars &
never let go.!

Helen

From Foster to Fabulous

ONE LITTLE GIRL'S JOURNEY THROUGH ABUSE,
FOSTER CARE, AGING OUT, AND LIFE BEYOND

Helen Ramaglia

Inspiring Voices®
A Service of Guideposts

And Then . . . God Sent Me You

There was a little girl,
so lonely, oh' so blue.

No one there to hold her,
or tell her, "I love you."

There was a little girl,
no happiness in sight.

No one there to run to,
full of emptiness inside.

There was a little girl,
alone and full of fright.

No one there to miss her,
or keep her warm at night.

There was a little girl,
so lonely, oh' so blue.

The heavens opened up,
and then...

God sent me you.

Written by Helen Ramaglia
For my foster parents

The cover of this book was drawn by Michael Ann
Bellerjeau
www.thedwellingplacegallery.com

The little girl is a drawing of me at 3½ years old
wearing the dress I wore to my mother's funeral. The
little bird represents the baby bird that died in my hands
during one of the lowest moments in my life.

The drawing of the lady in the mirror is me today.
I hold my hands out as a grown dove takes flight. The
dove represents my dreams. The mirror represents the
confinement of the abused foster child, and effects
of it into adult life. The bird flying out of the mirror
represents my dreams and the ability to *finally* allow
them to take flight -- my ability to *finally* break the
barrier and confinement of my past.

Inspiring Voices books may be ordered through booksellers or by contacting:

Inspiring Voices
1663 Liberty Drive
Bloomington, IN 47403
www.inspiringvoices.com
1-(866) 697-5313

Because of the dynamic nature of the Internet, any web addresses or links contained in this book may have changed since publication and may no longer be valid. The views expressed in this work are solely those of the author and do not necessarily reflect the views of the publisher, and the publisher hereby disclaims any responsibility for them.

Any people depicted in stock imagery provided by Thinkstock are models, and such images are being used for illustrative purposes only.

Certain stock imagery © Thinkstock.

ISBN: 978-1-4624-0293-9 (sc)
ISBN: 978-1-4624-0294-6 (e)

Library of Congress Control Number: 2012914942

Printed in the United States of America

Inspiring Voices rev. date: 08/27/2012

Contents

THE FOSTER YEARS

~~~~~~~~

"Smile despite the circumstances

and laugh throughout the pain.

Life is full of hardships,

but it is how you deal with them

that will, in the end,

define you."[1]

[1]   Author Unknown

Chapter 1

One of the most important tests in my life occurred last year. I had pushed myself out of my comfort zone and volunteered for Xtreme Life Camp, a faith-based camp for foster children. I didn't tell the children at camp that I was a prior foster child because I wanted to be sure I could work with them without my past getting in the way emotionally. You see, I tend to get emotional anytime I even mention the word "foster."

When we returned to the church from camp, I was in a bathroom stall and overheard a conversation between one of our foster campers and her foster mother. It went something like this:

Foster child: Mom, I don't want to take that medication any more. It makes me shaky all over and it's hard to walk. I can't talk when I take it, and it makes me a little drunk.

Foster mother: I don't care how it makes you feel! You're going to keep taking it, no matter what. You don't talk back when you take it!

The foster mother was caught off guard when I walked out of the bathroom stall. We were the only three in the bathroom. As the foster mother went into one of the stalls, I washed my hands and then I looked at the little girl. I said to her, "Did you know I used to be a foster child?" She immediately teared up and said, "*YOU* used to be a foster child? …But you're so put together!" I teared up and said, "YES, *I* used to be a foster child just like you. It's O.K..…You're going to be okay." Then I took her face in my hands and I said, "Sweetie, you reach for the stars and don't you let go. YOU are beautiful, and YOU are fabulous. YOU can be anything you want to be." I hugged her and we shed a couple of tears. Her foster mother came out of the stall and looked at me. As I left, I stood at the door and said once again to the little girl, "Remember, *anything* is possible." Then I found the closest, private corner I could find inside of that really big church and I cried. I sat down on the floor and cried like a baby!

When you put a foster child together with a prior foster child adult, the reaction is one that brings tears to my eyes every time. Just the mere thought of this brings tears to my eyes. The life of a foster child is so unbelievably traumatic that only another foster child can understand the deep endless pit of emptiness, loneliness and helplessness. It's a pain so deep that words don't exist, and only another foster child can understand it. The life of a foster child is so horrible that, when a current foster child meets a prior foster child who's grown and has made something of their life, all they can do is cry for each other. Words aren't always shared; but the tears, they're always there. It's such a relief to finally see and hold someone who truly understands and knows how horrible, empty and miserable you feel inside. The prior foster child cries for the lost child that never was and because they know the endless pain and treacherous journey that still lies ahead for the child in front of them. The foster child cries for the life they feel they may never have and the realization that, finally, there is someone else who truly knows how terribly empty their heart is and the hopelessness they feel every single day. The foster child cries with relief that, although they've heard behind their back they will never succeed, here -- standing in front of them -- is a foster child who did make it. The foster child cries for the fear inside that keeps them from seeing themselves in the prior foster child's shoes, the fear that although they desperately want to be the prior foster child, they truly don't feel they have it within themselves but they desire it so badly that they can taste it. However, they dare not allow themselves to even think it a possibility because they know they couldn't bear another hurt or another failure. They are afraid that this hurt, this failure, just might be that "one more" that will cause them to fizzle out, to go into that world where only the insane go.

While a foster child, I never could have imagined the life I have today. I don't think foster children ever feel they have much potential;

therefore, they tend to limit their dreams. I know I did. I never realized I could reach for the stars and truly get there. Therefore, I never risked dreaming big. Actually, I never risked dreaming at all. Working with foster children, I see this all the time.

To help you understand, imagine that you are a child, a very young child – say 6 years old. You are living with one parent. The other parent either died or deserted you several years ago. It doesn't really matter which; to a child, either one carries the emotional scar of desertion. Your remaining parent is often drunk or on drugs, rages at you and your siblings, and inflicts bodily and emotional injury from time to time. You're never quite sure what will make him or her angry, so you're always very careful in what you say and do. You walk on eggshells each and every day. But it doesn't matter. The rage can easily be provoked by someone else and turned on you in an instant. You withdraw and your emotions become numbed. You become a living, breathing "shell of a child." You can't concentrate on learning the things other children learn at this age; your focus is merely survival.

However, you love your parent. They're not *always* angry, and their love is the only kind of love you know. It's *all* you know, and it's your security. Your bond with your siblings is strong because together you face the dangers of home life. They understand you; your dog understands you, too. Then, suddenly, you are ripped out of the life you know, separated from your parent and your siblings. Your head is spinning; you are devastated, shocked and crying. Strangers from the Department of Family and Children's Services (DFCS) stormed into your house and, with no explanation, gave you three minutes to grab what you could. This is now all you own. You had to leave behind your favorite doll, your favorite dress, the special shoes Grandma got you, your trophy from the spelling bee. All you own now is 2 pairs of pants and a few shirts you grabbed from the laundry basket, 2½ pairs of shoes because you couldn't find the mate to one quick enough. You weren't allowed to take any toys, and while in shock you forgot your favorite teddy bear. After all, you thought you would be back to go to bed in your own house. No one said you wouldn't be coming back or how long you would be gone. You're thinking a day, maybe two.

Alone, without your siblings, you find yourself being led by a stranger down the street in a strange town holding a small black garbage bag containing a few of your clothes and possessions. It's all you have. In the blink of an eye you no longer have family; you no longer have friends or your school; your dog is now gone from your life; and most of your prized possessions are gone . . . just like that. In the blink of an eye, everything you knew as life is now gone. In the blink of an eye, your life no longer exists. No goodbyes – just gone! You feel like the garbage your black bag represents.

The stranger with you knocks on the door of yet another stranger who takes you inside to a room where four other children sleep. You are told this is your bed. The other children see your bag, open it and take some of the few things you own. You stand there in shock wondering what in the world just happened. No one explains or comforts you. You don't know these people, but you are told they are now your mother and father. You have to call this woman you don't know "Mom" and this man "Dad." There are all new rules to follow now, and you have no idea what most of them are. You walk on eggshells every day because you don't know when this nightmare is going to end or if this same scenario will repeat tomorrow. You even sense that this new Mom and Dad are more interested in the money the State provides their household than in your wellbeing, growth and development. You are treated as an "ordinary" child, and your new world expects you to act normally. Yet, you're in so much distress that you no longer talk. But . . . you are quiet, so it's easy for everyone to pretend there is no problem. No attempt is made to help you overcome the trauma of abuse and the trauma of foster care life, to encourage you, to nurture you, to teach you about life.

This 'foster life' will become your new life until the "lucky" day you age out. At that point, you get a $500 check and are told you are now on your own. With the tick of a clock at midnight on your eighteenth birthday, you are expected to shoulder your emotional baggage, find your way in the world, and successfully navigate the challenges and responsibilities of adulthood. Will you succeed?

My name is Helen Ramaglia, and I have lived the traumas of abuse and the foster care system. Believe me, foster care is TRAUMATIC!!!!!! The foster child spends every day merely surviving, many walking around as empty shells, not knowing real love or care.

While my story is not unique, I want to share it in order to help the caring people of America walk in the shoes of a child who experiences physical, mental and emotional abuse, is removed from everything she knows, is provided a roof over her head by the State and strangers, and then is thrust into adulthood totally unprepared . . . but later succeeds. I want to take them as close as possible to see, touch and feel what the abused/foster child suffers and why they are who they are. I want them to see the major gaps in the child's life skills and social abilities and why they exist. We must walk in the child's shoes in order to understand them. Only then will we be able to truly fill the enormous amount of needs they have and feel confident in adopting, fostering and working with foster children.

I want to tell DFCS about foster children and how they feel about being pushed around as pawns. I want them to see how much trauma they add to a child already in a state of crisis and educate them on the need to intensely coach foster parents and social workers on how to understand their foster children, fill their empty shells, and overcome the devastation in their lives. Sadly, this need still exists today. I know because the two foster children my husband and I have adopted were in a deeper state of crisis when they arrived in our home than I was 40 years ago.

I also want to show America that a child from this horrible state of crisis can still, indeed, bloom into a beautiful rose. They are not to be feared, but embraced. Is it hard? YES . . . but it's absolutely worth the ride! Foster children are not ordinary people -- they are extraordinary people!

I share my story to inspire the foster child to reach for the stars, to look inside and correct behaviors that need correcting on their own, to accept responsibility for their own tomorrows and not be defined by their past. They can overcome and become phenomenal . . . if they want it bad enough.

Yes, there is hope! My life now is extraordinary, but I can assure you that the journey to this place was not easy. I fell MANY times and it took decades to get here, but eventually I made it. It took me over 40 years to find the woman I am today, but it is my hope that this book will serve to make the path for today's foster children a lot easier and lead to success.

I invite you now to walk awhile in my shoes . . .

Chapter 2

On July 5, 1962 on the side of the road, under a bridge, in the back seat of a neighbor's car a tiny, feisty little girl was born, a fragile little baby tiny enough to live in a shoe box. Even then I was stubborn, stubborn and determined, determined to do things my way, determined to survive. However, that stubbornness and determination would be my salvation. Without it, I never would have made it --not as the person I am today, anyway.

I have no idea what I weighed at birth or how early I was. All I know is that I have always been told I was very, very tiny. My father loved telling the story of my birth. I sat mesmerized every time he talked about it. My father said he delivered me and that he spanked me all the way to the hospital. He said he didn't know he was supposed to cut the umbilical cord but that he remembered watching people spank new babies on TV to make them cry. I never asked any questions (I didn't talk much), but I would sit and hang onto every word of this incredible story. Each time he told this story, in my mind I would imagine a wonderful picture of him lovingly tending to me. It was as if I could feel my father's heart and love for me in each and every word.

The story of my birth in the car under the bridge made the South Carolina newspaper. My first day of life and I'm already making sure I'm in the spotlight, quietly doing something different to make sure I get noticed. Years later, in my adult life, my half-sister showed me the article that was published about my birth. In the article it said my grandmother was there with my mother. My father was obviously absent from the whole ordeal. It was then that I realized my father had concocted the whole story and mesmerized me all those years with a lie. What kind of man could fabricate such an intricate lie about one of life's most precious moments? My father later corroborated that he wasn't present. He never acknowledged the lie he had told my entire life about my birth but only said, "No, I wasn't there." It felt as if he had slapped me as hard as he could that day and then walked away as if it never happened.

Throughout my childhood, through all of the horror and trauma, I would always go back to that story and feel my father's tenderness and love. It became the foundation of the relationship between my father and I. Then, all of a sudden, I found out that it was nothing but a lie. I remember getting a very sick feeling in the pit of my stomach because I suddenly realized how sick my father truly was. The story that got me through some of the toughest times of my childhood was all a lie. The day I was born, my father was out drinking and running around with other women. He was the same man the day I was born as the man he was the day the courts took me away from him. The courts had to take me and my siblings away and lock us up in a juvenile detention center to keep him from causing extreme harm or death to us. This is the kind of man my father was.

On the other hand, from the stories I was told, my mother was a hard working, beautiful, petite and soft spoken French woman. She died when I was 3 years old. I don't remember her or anything about her. I can't even remember the way she smelled. All I know is what I've been told. No one ever really talked about her throughout my life, so I don't really know much about her. I craved to hear any little word about her, but there were so few spoken. I would see pictures of her sometimes, but even very few of those existed. For some reason, everything about her seemed as if it was on a need-to-know basis only. My mother died at the young age of 29 from a brain tumor. That's what I had been told as a young child, anyway. Years later I would find out that that, too, was a lie.

My father was a violent alcoholic. He stopped drinking for a couple of years, but for the majority of his life he was a dedicated alcoholic. Drinking was what he did best. It was his career of choice. The only thing he did better than drinking was being mean. Don't get me wrong, he did have his nice moments; however, those were few and far between. There were some good moments the two years when he didn't drink. During those two years he managed to buy a new house, new car and a new boat. He even managed to hold onto a wonderful new wife . . . for a little while, at least. But, it didn't take long for the good life to get old.

Years later, in my adult life, when I finally had the opportunity to reconnect with my older biological sister, she told me a story about my father that would rock my world. Dottie was 8 years old when I was born, so she remembers things I don't. She told me that my father was not my real father. Dottie told me about a man that my mother had loved and was planning to leave my father for. She said that "this man" was my father. She said it in such a way that I believe every word she said. As she talked of this man, questions that my father's sisters had asked me throughout my childhood began to make sense. They questioned my wavy hair; they questioned the fact that I wore glasses when none of my siblings or family did; they questioned many things about me and I had never understood why --not until then. Suddenly it all made sense. It made sense why I was so different from my brother and my sister, Vicky. It made sense why there were baby pictures of all the children except for me. I believed her. Even now, I believe her story. I've even spoken to others who say they know that story to be true. Dottie said my "real father" died of a heart attack before my mother could leave my father and go to him. After hearing her story, I was so relieved. I was relieved that I didn't have my father's vile and evil blood running through my veins. I was so thankful to know that I wouldn't have to worry all my life if I would turn out like him. Dottie's story set me free because I truly feel my father must have had some type of mental illness. I truly do. He was such an evil man and hurt so many people. It was also a relief to know that I was created from love and happiness. Although I was the product of an adulterous affair, at least I was created out of love and happiness.

Today, life is different. Today I have battled the beast and have made it to that "other place." I have done my time in purgatory, and now it is time for me to open those terrible doors into the past and share my horror. Today is the day. Yes, today is the day that I will finally set aside life and **make** myself take the time to delve into the pits of darkness. Today I will delve into the pits of darkness, of hopelessness and helplessness to bring forth a better tomorrow for today's forgotten children; to bring forth a better tomorrow for America's orphans, America's forgotten children, America's foster children; and finally blow open America's dirty little secret. Here it is: America, there are orphans in your backyard. Do you know there are thousands and thousands of orphans in your own backyard? All over America hundreds of thousands of children have no parents. We call them "foster children," but they are orphans. When we see pictures of children overseas labeled "orphans," we think, "Aw... that poor little child!" and our hearts bleed for them. However, in America we aren't allowed to show pictures of them and we label them "foster children." Our hearts don't bleed for them; instead, our first instinct is to cringe and think hopeless, negative thoughts about them. These are innocent little children who have done nothing to cause the reason for their situation. America likes to think these children don't hear their negative slurs, but they do. I'm telling you, they hear it, they see it and they feel it every day, every single day. I heard it every day when I was in foster care and it followed me. Yes, those negative thoughts and feelings about that label I wore, "foster child," followed me into adulthood. As I work with foster children through my charity and other charities, I hear some of the same stories from today's foster children. As I work with them and watch them, I see the effects this has on their self-esteem and self-confidence, as was the case with me.

Do you know that after I became a foster parent and a potential foster adoptive mother, that label still followed me? Not only did it follow me, but it followed my two precious little foster boys as well. When people found out my husband and I were in the process of adopting them, they immediately asked, "Are you sure you want to do that? What about all the baggage? Aren't you afraid that when they get older....?" It was as if they felt the need to shake me into reality and warn me of impending disaster. However, I typically came back with, "Well, I just figure, since I was a foster child too, that we have the same baggage." Yeah....I think you can imagine the look of embarrassment on most of those faces. It's rather funny though, now that the adoption is final, the reaction is completely different. Now it's as if they view me as Mother Teresa, and then comes the "Do they have any issues?" question. I then explain that I was a prior foster child and this was the only way I would adopt. After they realize I was a foster child, it seems as if they are thinking, "Wow, foster children *can* become normal productive members of society!" Then they often ask for further information about adopting from the foster care system. Someone always knows someone else who has been trying to adopt but . . .; or often times they have been thinking about the idea of themselves adopting but the cost makes it prohibitive; or the horror stories they have heard about failed adoptions and the thousands of lost dollars become a huge emotional and financial hurdle. After they see with their own eyes that foster children can become normal children, they are suddenly open to discussing foster adoption. Amazing, huh? All merely due to a lack of "foster education."

When people look at my life and how far I have come, they tend to view the label of "foster child" differently. Now that I have come full circle in the foster world by adopting foster children, run a nonprofit which I founded for foster children, volunteer with partner organizations for foster children, speak at fundraisers, and advocate for foster children, people's opinion about me being a prior foster child is very different. However, the sad part about this is that before I had "proven" myself normal and able, before they ever got to know the woman I am inside, people judged me harshly merely because I wore that label. Merely because I was a "foster child," I had to work 150% harder most of my life for people to see me as "normal," before people let down their guard and viewed me as a capable adult, an adult without crippling "baggage." For years I never let people know I was a prior foster child -- I only told them after they got to know me and enjoyed the woman I am inside. When I would finally tell them I was a prior foster child, only then did my label become invisible.

Unfortunately, due to my lack of critical life and social skills, it took over 40 years for me to become the woman I am today. I look back and shed tears because there was so much wasted time. If someone had just stepped forward and taken me under their wing to fill the many gaps in my life skills and social abilities, just think what I could have done with my life. If I have managed to claw my way to where I am today by myself, just think of the possibilities if someone had mentored me, guided me, coached me....believed in me. If someone had just **believed in me**! My goodness -- the possibilities could have been endless.

God's children are in pain. They are hurting and we aren't helping them. God commands us to care for the orphans and widows in distress, so why are there thousands of foster children with unmet needs. Why are there thousands of children wanting nothing more than to just feel loved! I hear it time and time again: "I just wish someone loved me"; "I wish I didn't feel so alone"; "I feel all dark inside and I don't know how to make it go away." We aren't helping God's children. We are leaving them to fend for themselves; and then when they make a mistake, we blame them for it. If we don't like the way our children are turning out, then we need to do a better job at parenting! America, these are our children and we aren't taking care of our children.

So.... they dare not dream of life beyond the life they already live. I know --I've been there!

I sit here and I look at my life and I can't believe it's my life. Ordinary people don't have lives like this. This kind of life exists only in movies or in books; however, this is my life and it is real. I sit here and I am crying about the horrors of yesterday, yet am amazed at who and where I am today. How did this happen? How could a little girl so battered and traumatized have such an awesome and amazing life? If you don't believe in God... today is the day. You don't get from there to here without divine intervention. It's not possible. This is not a rags to riches story, this goes so much deeper. It's the impossible, becoming possible. Only God can create miracles, and I am a miracle. I feel like I'm God's little miracle. After all, he was the only one who was there for me through thick and thin. Only God loved me unconditionally and He didn't judge me the way man judged me. He believed in me when America didn't deem me worthy.

God …. He is my father and my best friend. He is my confidant and my hero. He is my teacher. He laughs with me and cries with me. He heals me and He wipes away my tears. He is there when I'm alone, and He waits patiently when I forget He's there. He's all knowing and all giving. He pushes me when I need pushing, and He lets me fall when I need humbling. His love is unconditional and His love is everlasting. But sometimes it's hard when your only father is an invisible father, especially when you are a child…. a foster child.

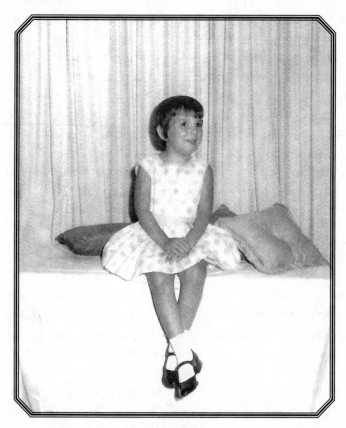

Me - About a year after my mother's death

Chapter 3

My mother, Diane Gaye Charbonneau Hall, was born on December 20, 1936. I have been told she was a beautiful French woman, that she was tall, thin, quiet and sweet. I have a picture of her in my living room and in the picture she's beautiful. She has very dark hair, is wearing red lipstick, and is obviously an impeccable dresser. She comes across as very sophisticated and elegant. I'm always impressed with how regal she seems because I know that's far from true. I've always wondered how she managed to pull off such an exquisite look knowing she comes from such humble beginnings. You would never know that from looking at her picture. From what I can gather, my mother's family was French immigrants, uneducated and extremely poor. I also know that when my mother died, her family's relationship with us died as well. It always seemed rather disturbing to me that my mother's family never saw us or talked with us after my mother's death. How could an entire family write off little children like that, especially knowing the horrible evil that lurked inside of the man who caused the death of this young, beautiful woman? I never understood how they could just walk away to never return or inquire about us, leaving us in his care.

As I study my mother's picture, I often look directly into her eyes and wonder what it would be like to have her here with me today. I wonder what it would feel like to have her arms around me giving me one of those enormous hugs you see moms and children exchange every day or what it would be like to call her on the phone when I need advice, comfort, or someone to share a laugh. Then I try with everything I have in my body to remember something about her; but no matter how hard I try, I can't remember anything. I look into those eyes and I try to feel her in my heart, but there's nothing. Sometimes I pick up her picture and ever so gently stroke her face as I look longingly into her eyes and wonder about this woman who I've been told is my mother. Sometimes, as I stare into her beautiful eyes, I shed tears. Tears of a relationship that never was, tears that I will never experience the intense love that only a mother can give.

Mother was only on this wonderful earth for 29 short, mostly violent years. Why would she stay and endure pain and suffering? To provide for her children. Years after her death, I reconnected with my older sister and had the opportunity to hear stories about my past. They were stories so horrible, so unbelievable, that I wanted to cover my ears and hum beautiful music while shaking my head. Inside I cried, "No, no, no! This can't be! This can't be my life. This can't be my mother. This *cannot* be my life she's talking about!" Yet, I desperately yearned to know what this poor woman went through to keep her babies safe. I needed to know; I needed to understand. Although I couldn't feel her love no matter how hard I tried, in listening to these gut-wrenching words, I knew she must have loved us dearly to have endured the life she had to endure to care for us. My mother must have loved me so much. My mother loved me so much that she died for me. For three years of my life, I was loved, truly loved. I was loved *unconditionally* for three very short years.

The day my mother died my father became the proud owner of 4 children. Dottie was 12 at the time; Danny was about 6, my sister Vicky was 4, and I was 3. Four children my father never really wanted, at least that's what his actions said. If it wasn't for my mother, we wouldn't have eaten, had clothes or had a roof over our heads. I have no idea what my father did for a living at the time or if he even worked.

For many years I would see a vague picture in my mind, a faint memory unconnected to an event. Over and over, I'd remember running and yelling, "Mommy!" I didn't understand it throughout my childhood; but later in life when I met my oldest sister, Dottie, she said that when the hearse took our mother away to bury her, I was running after the hearse crying and yelling, "Mommy! Mommy!

I want my Mommy!" She said I ran and then fell down on my bottom crying for my mother. I don't remember anyone picking me up and consoling me. I'm sure someone did, but I didn't ask Dottie that question. We were both too choked up to speak any further about it.

After my mother was buried, it's been said by many, that the cemetery owner and his wife wanted to adopt all four of us children. I was told that my grandmother refused because she didn't want anyone to adopt us. She didn't want to take care of us, but she didn't want anyone to adopt us either. I've been told she was receiving government checks for us; and if someone adopted us, she would no longer be eligible for them. I do know that she called an aunt and uncle to come and get us. I have an uncle who is paralyzed, and they were having problems getting pregnant. So, my grandmother asked them (actually, from what I hear, she told them) to come and get us. If you knew my grandmother, you would understand that, yes, she probably did tell them instead of asking them. Our family was very different. It was a very cold, unloving environment. I tried to love my grandmother, but she was very hard to love. It was hard to get into her heart. I know she had one -- I just couldn't feel it. My grandmother's eyes were empty. I think there must have been a lot of pain in her own childhood.

The Aunt and Uncle my grandmother called were already in the process of adoption when we became available. They had to go pick up their little bundle before they could take us. I'm not sure of the time lapse, but we stayed with my grandmother until they picked us up. During this time, my father's sister took in our Dottie. She was old enough to help clean and would be more of an asset than a burden. My brother stayed with my grandmother, but my sister and I were too young and no one wanted us. So off to my Aunt and Uncle's house we finally went. We moved from Columbia, South Carolina, where Dottie and Danny were living to Warner Robins, Georgia. I could never understand how family could so easily split up four siblings like that. I'm sure my sister Vicky and I were quite a handful. A couple with no children now suddenly had a new baby and two little ones, all under 5 years of age. They probably weren't prepared for us, and I'm pretty sure their lives were turned upside down. Living with my

Aunt and Uncle was a lot of fun. It felt like a real home. Because my mother was often times very sick with headaches when I was small, my sister Dottie pretty much took care of us, especially me. I was the baby. Dottie said that I was so small and delicate as a baby that she pretended I was her baby doll. However well intentioned my very loving mother was, she was not physically able to provide us with a real home environment. She worked very hard no matter how ill she was, and for that I will always love and have the highest respect for her. However, this was our first real family experience.

I have no idea where my father was or what he was doing at the time. As always, he wasn't taking care of his children. So, there we were with my Aunt and Uncle which, to be honest, was actually a blessing. My sister was in school, but I wasn't old enough yet. Instead, I was allowed to take dance lessons. I felt like a little ballerina. I had always been a very small and petite child, so I think I probably made a great ballerina, at least at that age I thought I did. I enjoyed tap dancing best. I felt really special when I got to put on my little black shiny shoes and make those little tap noises. When I was dancing, I felt like I was in heaven and was dancing with the angels. I loved to get out there in front of the people and dance for them. I was so happy and so proud --I felt like a princess. Nothing existed when I was dancing. It was just me, the music, the movements and my dreams. I thought I was very good at it and I loved it. Although I was only 4 years old, it felt great to feel so free and happy. I think this was the very first time I had ever felt safe in my young little life.

Another thing I was good at was saving money. In my mind I can still see my amber colored piggy bank. Even as a little girl I loved saving money. My Aunt and Uncle still tell the story of how we were away from home and someone had given me a coin for my piggy bank. They said that when we got home I was the only one with my coin and that I had held it so tightly and for so long that I had the impression of the coin still in my hand after I put it in the piggy bank. This was a trait that would serve me well in my adult life.

I will never forget the story of our neighbor who grew beautiful, large award-winning tomatoes. My sister and I went next door to our neighbor's garden and picked his beautiful red tomatoes. We picked almost all of them and ate them. Our neighbor's complaint wasn't that we picked and ate them; it was that we took one big bite out of each tomato and then got another. We did that until his tomatoes were all ruined. Then reality set in; horror hit home. My Aunt and Uncle made me break open, yes, break open my treasured piggy bank and give our neighbor all of the money I had saved. Boy did that hurt! I shed many tears that night. It broke my heart to give that man all of the money in my piggy bank.

My Aunt and Uncle had a pool installed in their backyard while we were living with them. You know, one of those above ground, rather large ones in our very own backyard. We were so proud of our new pool. One night we were allowed to get inside the pool while the hose was filling it up. It was night and I remember being under the stars. I remember laughing and having a great time. I loved the water -- I found it so calming. That night, in the water as we played and floated, nothing existed except floating in the calmness, under the stars with nothing to think about except my dreams and our new life of fun. It was so much fun walking around in the water and playing games that night. We played like normal children with normal lives and went to bed exhausted from all the play. I'm sure we slept well.

The next day when we went into the pool I was shocked and amazed. I couldn't understand how it happened, how in the world it was that I was able to walk around in the pool the night before but the next day couldn't even begin to reach the bottom. The water was so much deeper. Something that was so much fun the night before had become work overnight. I learned to swim in no time at all. Next to the love of dancing was now the love of swimming. I found the water to be very calming, and I loved spending as much time as I could in the pool.

When we lived with my Aunt and Uncle we were allowed to have a duck. This duck was our very first pet. I remember going outside and feeding the duck and playing with him. I remember feeling almost like a normal little girl and having fun like normal little girls are supposed to.

19

I also remember getting spanked for wetting the bed while we lived there. My sister and I shared a bed, and every morning my side of the bed would be wet and I would get a spanking. My Aunt said that it seemed odd that every morning I had to go to the bathroom but my sister didn't. After they had gotten bunk beds for us, they realized that it was my sister wetting the bed and not me. My sister would pull down her panties, come to my side of the bed and potty. So every morning it looked like I was the one wetting the bed and not her. After we got our own beds, they realized what had been going on.

Summer gave way to winter and one day it snowed. I don't think I had ever seen snow before. I remember my Aunt going outside, getting snow and making ice cream from the snow. It tasted so good. I don't remember playing in the snow, but I'm sure we did. I just remember eating that terrific snow ice cream.

For the first time in our lives, we were children. We didn't have to be scared everyday wondering when that awful, evil man was going to walk in the door. We didn't have to watch the horrible things he did to my mother. We didn't have to cry and watch as he beat up on his children. We didn't have to listen to the screaming, yelling and profanity. We didn't have to watch him throw and break anything and everything we owned. We were finally able to just be children. It felt so wonderful to finally be a child that I don't remember missing my mother or my big sister.

Then, one day out of the blue, wonderful news came: My sister Dottie was coming for a visit! I was so happy; she was like a Goddess to me. I adored her and it had been so long since I had seen her. I was so excited; after all, she practically raised me. After she arrived, I remember Vicky and I were swimming in the pool and playing Marco Polo with Dottie. I thought it was so much fun because she always had trouble finding us. My Aunt noticed she would always go in the same direction no matter where we hollered from. Come to find out, she was deaf in one ear. My father had slapped her so hard that he busted her eardrum when she was a young child. The damage was irreversible, and she would always be deaf in one ear because of that horrible man. Because we hadn't seen my dad since the death of my mother, she had to have been under 11 when he did that to her.

The day came when Dottie had to go back to my aunt's house in South Carolina. Sometime shortly after that we were sent back to my grandmother's house. My Aunt and Uncle had wanted to adopt us and needed parental rights to legally provide for us. Adoption was an anchor of stability that everyone needed if they were going to be the ones raising us. My grandmother wouldn't agree, so we were sent back. Although my grandmother didn't want to raise us, she didn't want to give up my father's legal rights either. That decision caused a split between my Aunt and Uncle and the rest of the family that would last into my adult life.

After one year of living with my Aunt and Uncle we had to move away, leaving the only sense of family and stability we had ever known. Two families had wanted to adopt us and keep us together; twice they had been turned down. Those decisions were made for personal selfish reasons, and it was the children who were hurt. Lost were the things I loved most: my mother, my oldest sister, my brother, my Aunt and Uncle, the dancing and the swimming. Gone was the carefree frolicking fun of little children. Gone was my short lived childhood—but one year was better than nothing. Some children don't even get that much.

My beautiful mother
Diane Gaye Charbonneau Hall

Chapter 4

Over the river and through the woods, to Grandmother's house we go....

After we were sent back to South Carolina, we lived with my grandmother and Grandpa Drake. Grandpa Drake was my step grandfather. My real grandfather died before I was born and I never knew anything about him. My grandmother lived in a house across from the school. It was Grandpa Drake's house and I remember him having a warehouse, or something like that, across the street from the house. I remember us going over there with him and looking around. We spent a lot of time outside, in the warehouse and across the street in the school playground. We had a lot of fun living with my grandmother. Grandpa Drake was fun to be with. Although we enjoyed living at our grandmother's, there was very little affection or guidance. A day with Grandmother was more about being scolded for negative things, but positive things were rarely pointed out. There were few hugs and it wasn't a warm environment. I also don't recall her playing, laughing or teaching us anything. We were merely children left to entertain ourselves with little if any adult interaction.

I will never forget the night my father came over to my grandmother's house. I remember two women in his car and very loud music playing. Dad must have come to pick us up to show us off to his "girl of the moment" when all of a sudden Grandfather Drake and my dad got into a fist fight. Dad was drunk as usual, and Grandpa wasn't going to let him take us with him. I remember Grandpa Drake getting a frying pan and hitting Dad in the head with it. I remember a lot of blood and a woman screaming in the car while loud music blasted away. Dad finally left and we were tucked safe and sound into our beds. I don't remember living with Grandmother very long after that before she found another family to keep us.

Grandmother let us live with a family who lived on the other side of the school. I remember staying with the older son in the afternoons because kindergarten was only a half day and my brother and sister went to school all day. I remember him taking flour that was inedible and us making dough outside to play with. We made pretend cakes and biscuits. I enjoyed pretending we were cooking, and then we had a pretend picnic outside to eat the pretend food we had prepared. We always had so much fun playing together. He was a lot of fun and he loved to play little kid games with me. I also remember him sitting me on his lap and touching me in my panty area. He never did anything to hurt me, but he liked playing that game a lot. Being a little girl, I thought it was just a game or kids' play and thought nothing more of it. As a child, you are merely happy your friends like playing with you and that you are making them happy. I never thought there was anything wrong with that kind of play or those kinds of games.

One morning when we lived at their house, I remember stepping on the porch to wave goodbye to my sister as she walked down the sidewalk to school. I remember it being a very foggy morning and the air being cold and damp. It felt very eerie outside. I don't remember ever seeing fog before that day And I was very scared. I was frantically screaming and crying and yelling that the fog would eat her if she went into it and she'd never come back. I held onto her arm and tried to pull her back onto the porch, crying, begging and pleading for her to please stay. She left anyway. I remember everyone laughing at the humor of it all. To me it wasn't funny -- I was terrified. As she stepped into the fog, she disappeared; and I was so scared that I passed out. I think at that point they probably stopped laughing. All they had to do was explain the fog to me. If they had just taken a few minutes to show me that the fog was safe, all of the drama could have been avoided. The scars of that episode never left.

I think I may have felt that my mother was taken away, my oldest sister was taken away, my father didn't want us, we were taken from my Aunt and Uncle in Warner Robins, and my grandmother didn't want us. I thought the fog had eaten my sister and now I had no one. I don't remember Danny being in this picture, so either I was totally focused on my sister, or he too had been taken away. It was a terrifying moment for me. I don't think anyone ever understood how traumatic this was. No one was able to empathize with my loss nor did they attempt to understand my feelings. I was a 5 year old little girl who had already suffered more trauma and loss than most of them would experience in a lifetime.

As always, this family didn't last very long and we moved to yet another family. All of these families that we were living with were not part of our family, but merely acquaintances of my grandmother who wanted to keep little children who needed a home. This time we went to live with a couple in Cayce, South Carolina. I remember him being in a wheelchair, and I think he was a preacher. I think I remember Danny being there for a little while. There seemed to be a pattern that every time we went to live somewhere new, Danny would come too; but it was never very long before he would leave. I have no idea where he went, and there was never any conversation or opportunity to say goodbye. It was merely one day he's here and the next day he's not.

I remember when we lived with the preacher and his wife, a free ball came with a bottle of Mr. Clean she had purchased. I remember my sister and I playing with the ball in our bedroom. I threw the ball up in the air and it hit the light fixture. It broke and the pieces came tumbling down. As the pieces landed, one of them hit the top of my nose and cut it pretty badly. When the preacher's wife came in, I immediately blamed it on my sister. I think I was afraid of getting into trouble. I remember the preacher's wife saying it was okay and tending to the wound. I remember thinking how nice she was for not spanking me. I just *knew* I was going to get a spanking for that. I don't remember going to the hospital or the doctors or the stitches, but I remember a lot of blood and a pretty bad cut.

My favorite time with this family was Christmas. This was the first Christmas I could remember having when I was young. I remember my sister and I getting an Easy Bake oven. I was so happy and tickled with our Easy Bake oven. I couldn't believe it actually baked real cakes. I thought it was pretty awesome to bake my own cake and even more awesome when I got to spread icing on the cake. I baked a chocolate cake with chocolate icing and it tasted really good. I remember being so happy that Christmas. I remember being happy living with them . . . for the most part.

However, during this span of my life, I remember a couple of things that seem odd. I don't remember another family after this family, but the events I remember seemed odd for a preacher and his wife. So here are the events. Either we lived with another family before going to live with my dad, or this indeed happened with this couple.

I remember being kept in a closet when they went off so that we would stay out of trouble. I remember being scared of the dark at first, but then I found it comforting. Maybe I thought that, at least in the closet, I was staying out of trouble and didn't mind it because it was making our "parents" happy.

I could be wrong, but I don't think I am. I remember the preacher's wife asking my sister to do something for her. I watched what she was doing and I remember I kept saying, "I wanna do it. I want a turn. It's my turn now!" Even then I was a people pleaser and wanted my "parents" to be happy with me. Now that I'm older I understand what was going on, but at that time nothing about it seemed dirty or out of place. We were children who were touched in private areas quite frequently so nothing about it seemed wrong. No one had ever discussed that we should never be touched there by people or that we shouldn't touch anyone there either. There was a time in my adult life where I would question if I were a lesbian because I participated in that act. However, in time I discarded that notion and accepted that I was merely a child being a child, being led by an adult who knew better. Once I came to terms with that, it no longer worried me. It would take years for me to realize that these fragments were indeed memories and not fabrication. They were vague memories that resurfaced for years until I came to terms with them. They didn't haunt me, they just were. When I became an adult, I had the opportunity to speak with my oldest sister, Dottie, and was able to corroborate that a couple of other stories had actually happened. Therefore, I feel this story, too, is indeed a fact. I am certain these vague memories are bits and pieces of events etched in my mind because of content and/or the impact they made on my life. I don't remember the time span with these families or if these were the only two families we lived with after coming back to my grandmother's, but I do know that we had moved around almost constantly since my birth. When my mother was alive and after she died, we lived in multiple places every year, except for the year we lived with my Aunt and Uncle in Warner Robins. That year was the longest span of time we were with any one family.

After the preacher's family, I remember being sent to live with my father and my new stepmother. It must have been during the end of my 1st grade year when we went to live with them, and I must have been about six at the time.

Dottie & My Grandmother
Me, Vicky & Danny
A few months after mother's death

27

Chapter 5

My Dad and our new stepmother, Glenda......Wow, I didn't know what to expect, how to feel or what to think. We were about to venture on a journey with the man who single handedly caused us years of trauma, pain and heartache. I felt as if we were being sent into the lion's den. How does a child prepare for something like that?

When we went to live with my dad and Glenda, life was different from what I expected . . . it was fun! I was completely surprised and baffled. This wasn't the same man who was married to my mother, but a different man, a man I had never seen before. Surprisingly, in time I would come to love and adore this man who I called "Daddy." How could it be that this was the same man I was so scared of, the man who terrified me to the point that I feared speaking? This was a man that any woman would love; and Glenda, she was such an amazing woman. Somehow I would find myself also adoring this woman I would call "Mom." Glenda was the only mother I knew because I couldn't remember anything about my real mother. Life with my parents was awesome; it was incredible. I finally had a normal life and I had real parents for the first time ever. For the first time ever, I was a normal little girl with normal parents living a normal little girl's life. I was so very happy and content. I wanted it to last forever, and there was nothing to make me think that life would ever be any different than it was at that moment. I was such a happy little girl.

When we first went to live with Dad and Glenda, we lived in a single-wide mobile home with my new mom; my adoring father; Glenda's two sons, Larry and Robbie; my middle sister, Vicky; Danny and me. Five kids and two adults in a two bedroom single-wide mobile home. It was a tight fit, but we didn't care. We were together; we were a family; and most of all, we were happy. We were a family.... what a strange word to me!!!!

Dottie was still missing from the picture, but life was good. We had wonderful days when we lived with Glenda. This was a life I had never known. Glenda had girlfriends and they visited each other's houses and would frost each other's hair. I remember them chatting, laughing and having a great time together. We kids would get money from Glenda and walk to the store to buy soda and candy. I remember the boys playing while my sister and I sat on the stairs and watched them play and have fun. Glenda used to come outside and tell Vicky and me that it was okay for us to play, that it was okay for us to get dirty. It took a while for Glenda to make it clear but, eventually, we believed her. After a lot of coaxing from Glenda, we started playing with the boys and pretty soon it became pretty much a daily routine. We just played, had fun and got all dirty. For the first time in our lives we were being normal kids in a normal family with a mother and a father, playing, having fun, and getting dirty like normal little kids are supposed to do.

It felt so good to finally be a normal family. Dad worked hard and he soon found a job where he earned enough money to rent a house. After we moved into a bigger house, Dottie came to live with us. I was so happy when Dottie came -- we were finally complete! We were all together and we were one big happy family. I just knew this was the start of something wonderful for us. After years of abuse, I could finally allow myself to enjoy life as it was supposed to be enjoyed. I couldn't get enough of my sister Dottie. I wanted to be around her all the time. I just knew life couldn't get any better than this. I followed Dottie everywhere and touched her as much as I could. I was so happy having her in my life again.

But shortly after Dottie came to live with us, suddenly, she was no longer there. As always, one day a sibling would be there and, without any advance warning or opportunity for goodbyes, the next day they would be gone. I never questioned this because it happened so frequently during our life that it just became normal. Thieves coming in the middle of the night and stealing a sibling was just a normal way of life for us. How sad.

I remember a little fighting between Dad and Glenda surrounding Dottie's departure, but it didn't last long. Dottie was sent to live with the same Aunt and Uncle who had kept me and my sister Vicky. After she was gone, things got back to normal. I would be an adult before I had the opportunity to talk to Dottie and find out what happened. I do know that whatever happened, Glenda and Dad had a bad fight. I didn't hear it, but Glenda woke us kids and took us to a neighbor's house. While she gathered us kids together, she kept trying to pull her pant leg up to see something that was obviously hurting her a lot. As she pulled her pant leg up, I saw this deep gouge in the shin of her leg and I asked what happened. She said she hurt it climbing over the bed. Deep in my heart and head, I knew my dad had something to do with it; and I remember getting a sick feeling in the pit of my stomach.

Glenda took us over to a girlfriend's house and we stayed the night with her. We either went home the next day or a couple of days later. Things were pretty quiet for quite some time and that sick feeling in the pit of my stomach left. I trusted this was a onetime thing and life was back to normal. I felt it was okay to let down my guard and just enjoy life as a little girl once again. Deep inside I missed Dottie. I wanted her back, but I was beginning to love Glenda like a mommy and that feeling went away after awhile.

Life went on as if nothing ever happened. I remember one afternoon Dad calling my spelling words out to me. I was typically good in school, but I think I must have been having a hard time focusing that day. My spelling words were three letter words, and Dad was getting really frustrated having to call them out to me over and over again. He finally got so frustrated that he spanked me . . . hard. The very next time he called them out, I got them correct. Dad's fix to everything was a "behind woppin" as he called it. Well, he called it something a little more vulgar, but we will just call it a "behind woppin." I think a "behind woppin" was the only problem solving technique Dad must have learned, because he used it for everything. He never attempted discussing, talking, teaching, or explaining . . . just a "behind woppin."

That year Santa brought my sister and I beautiful pink bikes for Christmas. I was thrilled, not only that we got bikes, but that they were pink. I loved the color pink and all throughout our childhood people would dress Vicky and I in the same outfits, typically one in pink and one in blue. Most of the time she would get the pink one and I would get the blue one. Although I felt like a princess anytime I got anything new and never complained, secretly I wanted the pink one really badly. I thought it was so dainty and feminine. So a pink bike was just what I needed to make me feel pretty.

One day as I was riding my new bike home from school, a little bully girl pushed me off my bike. I was minding my own business, eating a candy bar and enjoying the sweet taste of chocolate and the wind in my face when all of a sudden I fell to the ground. She made me drop three quarters of an uneaten chocolate bar, stole my bike and made me bite a big gash in my lip. So, with a fat bloody lip, scrapes and bruises I hobbled home crying. When my sister Vicky found out what had happened, she set out with a vengeance. Not only did she find my bike, but she made sure that little girl -- rather big next to me -- would never do that again. From that day forward, I rode my bike with my head held high, knowing that these fools knew I was untouchable. I had a big sister who could whip anyone's behind and they knew it!

After we went to live with Dad, the teachers in our new school couldn't understand what I was saying and made me take speech class in school, which I did for several years. The speech therapist said that I baby talked and we needed to work on my pronunciation. Shortly after working on my speech, I started stuttering. As time passed, I had a hard time talking without stuttering and Dad would constantly correct me. This actually made things much worse. It became clear that it was easier for me not to talk because he would get very angry with me when I stuttered. The more Dad corrected me, the worse my stuttering got; but he seemed oblivious to that. Dad said I was embarrassing him and he started slapping me every time I stuttered. So, one day I just stopped talking altogether. I didn't talk much anyway, so now I just didn't talk at all, unless I didn't have a choice. I just watched, listened and absorbed everything I could. But this was probably a good thing.

I learned at a very young age that, when it came to corporal punishment, Dad usually did things in an age/size order. Well, in both age and size, I was always last. Even though Glenda's son Robby was technically the youngest, I would usually still be last. I also learned at a very young age how to appeal to my father's ever-so-minute and very cold heart. In a very sweet, quiet, nice sort of way, I would start out pleading for the entire group as a whole; but in the end, it was my personal well being I valued most. I also hated pain and avoided it whenever possible. I figured that the others were capable of minor manipulation just as well as I was. So, when it actually came to "behind whoppin' time," as my dad called it, I figured it was every child for him or herself. I had a system. I would start out by trying to plead a lesser sentence for the group as a whole at the beginning of each misdeed. Then I would feel out negotiations and would cautiously weigh out how proceedings were going moment by moment. While in mid plea, I would determine whether to continue the group plea or change it to a single plea. If everything failed and negotiations were not going well even with a single plea, I would start crying as the first child got their spanking. I thought this show of empathy would hopefully make Dad see how truly sorry I was and things wouldn't be quite so harsh when he got to me. I hoped he would see I was so tender hearted and felt the others' pain so much that that in itself was enough without the spanking. I had hoped he would think that by having to watch the other 4 get their "behind whoppin" that I wouldn't need such harsh corporal punishment to learn the error of my ways. Sometimes, it actually worked!!!! Then there were other times when I could tell he was still going pretty strong and was already at Robby. Knowing I was next, now that was bad news. So, in a last ditch effort, when he would get to Robby, I would start bawling and boohooing. Sometimes, even though he wanted to spank me, he didn't. I figured, "Hey.... whatever works!" and "All is fair in love and war." But there were times when all efforts failed, and he spanked me anyway. However, I managed to get out of most of them. This typically caused some jealousy with my other siblings; but it wasn't about maintaining good sibling relations, this was about survival.

Things were going along pretty normally, well -- normally for my family -- until the day Danny threw a rock and hit me in the eye. I was in the second grade when this happened. I remember the white of my eye turning red and staying that way for several weeks. My dad wasn't someone who spent money on doctors unless he had no other choice. When my other eye started turning red, Glenda made my dad let her take me to the doctor. So, Glenda and all of us kids piled in the car and made our way to the doctor's office. After the doctor examined my eye, he sent us directly to a specialist's office and he, in turn, sent us directly to the hospital. I remember that by the time we made it to the hospital, Dad was with us and it was dark outside. The other kids were laying in the car all over each other asleep. I felt bad for them because it turned out to be an all day ordeal. Once I was admitted into the hospital, they made me stay flat on my back with patches over both of my eyes. I remember not being allowed to sit up, get out of bed, or even tilt my head up. For weeks they kept me flat on my back, not allowing me to get up for any reason, not even to go to the bathroom. They kept the bandages over both of my eyes for a very long time. Glenda's friends came to visit and brought toys that I could play with without using my eyes. The doctors were preparing me for one glass eye and possibly even going blind in the other. The doctors said that blood had pooled behind my eye and was bleeding over to the other eye. They said my optic nerve would be severely damaged from the trauma and that I might go blind in the other eye as well, and they talked to me about a glass eye.

Their words didn't impact me much, but the lying down and not getting to use my eyes impacted me a lot. After what seemed like several weeks in the hospital, they finally released me and Glenda took me home. Although the hospital released me, I would be limited to constant bed rest and patches over both of my eyes for a very long time. Glenda fed me, carried me to the bathroom and took care of me for months. She nursed me back to health; and during this time, she truly became My Mommy. I think I really needed this from her. I needed to be in a position where I had to depend on her for everything. This allowed me to truly love her like my mom. Because of this, Glenda and I were able to form a very close mother and daughter bond. I needed that so badly. I missed a lot of school, and Glenda fought for me when they made me repeat the 2nd grade for missing too many days. I was a very good student, but they couldn't allow me to advance to the next grade when I had missed most of the year. So, I repeated the 2nd grade; but it was worth it because Glenda took such good care of me and my eyes that I wouldn't have to get a glass eye after all. The doctors were amazed that my vision healed as well as it did. I remember them saying I was a walking miracle. At that age, I didn't understand the full impact of losing my eyesight or what it truly meant to have a glass eye. All I know is that when I got home from the hospital, the other kids were jealous of my toys; and it was only a few days before they were all torn up. I remember Danny cutting my doll open to see how she worked. You could pull a string and she would talk. I had never seen or had a doll that talked before, and it really hurt to lose her. The others were only angry with me for a little while, and it wasn't long before we were buddies again.

Soon after my eye incident, Dad and Glenda bought their very first house. It was a brand new house and it was beautiful. Shortly after Dad bought the house, he also bought a new boat and a new car. For the first time ever we were prospering. I remember getting toys and a coat for Christmas. Glenda and Dad seemed so happy. Dad was always pretty gruff with us kids, but that was just my dad. I loved Glenda so much that I rarely thought of Dottie anymore. I was building a great relationship with Robbie and especially with Larry. I actually had a better relationship with the two of them than I had with my biological brother and sister. Something about my brother and sister scared me. I was too scared of them to get close to them.

In the summer we would take trips to Knoxville, Tennessee, where Glenda's family lived. Glenda's parents were very poor, and they didn't have any running water in their house. I thought it was fun to live a different life for a little while there. Glenda's family treated us as if we had always been their grandkids and that was all that mattered to me. They were warm and loving, hugged us and loved on us; we were one big happy family. We loved being there. We had to pump water to take baths outside in a tin tub, and we had to go to the outhouse to use the bathroom. At night we all peed in a "pee pot," as MawMaw called it. Every morning she would get up and make homemade biscuits and bacon. I loved going to visit them -- it felt incredible to be loved and wanted by family.

The first summer we visited, they told us to stay out of the big empty drums; but we got inside of them anyway. We would crawl inside the drums and roll down the hills. We had a ball. Unfortunately, I cut my knee really badly on the sharp edge as I was getting out of a drum. I probably needed stitches, but we just bandaged it. I still have a pretty big scar from it. I thought I was going to get into trouble but Glenda just said, "That's O.K. Just go outside and play." And play we did. We explored the cliffs on the mountains. We frolicked and played from morning until night. We would play in the heat of the hot Tennessee summer, then take off our clothes and go skinny dipping in a hidden lake that no one probably knew existed. Because our clothes didn't get wet, Mom had no idea we had done that. We would swing in tire swings and roll inside of tires; we just played and played. We drank well water and ate down-home country cooking, enjoyed family and friends and ate watermelon. We were kids.

I would sing loudly to Helen Reddy and Tanya Tucker from the back seat of the car most of the way to Tennessee. Glenda and I would sing "Delta Dawn" and all of her other songs. Sometimes Glenda would let me sit in the front seat between her and Dad and we would sing together at the top of our voices. No one complained -- they enjoyed listening to us sing. Larry used to say I was a little songbird. He was so sweet to me, and I loved him as if he were my real brother instead of my step brother.

I'll never forget the day when Glenda went to the outhouse and all of a sudden we heard screaming. There was a snake in there with her! She came running out of the outhouse with her pants down around her ankles. She would squat down to finish peeing one minute and would stand up to pull her pants up the next and repeated each. She said she wasn't sure which to do -- finish peeing or pull her pants up and just pee in them. Needless to say, she wound up having to change her pants anyway. Dad heard her scream and ran outside, but he didn't do anything about the snake. He was just as scared of the snake as Glenda was. PawPaw finally took care of the snake. I think I remember him saying it wasn't poisonous. Everyone got a good laugh. I'm not sure if we laughed harder about Glenda running out with her pants around her ankles, or if we laughed harder at Dad being just as scared of the snake as Glenda was. I couldn't believe this violent man who had beat up on his wife and kids was afraid of a snake. I laughed and laughed until my side hurt.

Dad started coaching little league baseball and was a member of the volunteer fire department. I was amazed that this father was the same father that had beaten my real mother and us kids. In time, I finally let my guard down and allowed myself to fully enjoy this wonderful childhood I was having. There were many weekends that my dad took us kids to the racetrack while he sat with his volunteer fire buddies to watch the races. They had to be there just in case there was a fiery crash. We loved going with Dad and had a ball every time we went. Although I didn't care much for the gas fumes and the loud noises from the cars or the nasty bathrooms, it was fun. Some weekends he would take us fishing and sometimes we would just stay home and play.

I remember building a great relationship with Larry. He had the sweetest eyes. I remember when he smiled, his whole face would light up. I remember thinking that Larry was a very nice looking boy. His favorite treat was to lay on the couch and for me to rub his feet. Larry loved having his feet rubbed and he typically only let me rub them. The only thing better than me rubbing Larry's feet was for me to make him pickled onions. Larry would lie on the couch and eat pickled onions while I sat rubbing his feet. To Larry, this was his heaven on earth.

Glenda started playing bingo with her girlfriends and would take me and my sister with her. We must have been too much to handle together because in time she started taking us one at a time. I enjoyed going to play bingo with her; and every time I went, she would buy me Shirley Temples with lots of cherries in them. There was one day when Glenda won the jackpot; it was a lot of money. I remember her giggling when she got home and suddenly took all of the cash and just threw it up in the air. I remember putting my arms up and trying to catch as much of it as I could. Of course, I gave it all back. Dad and Mom were so happy. We kids were laughing and rolling around in it. I don't remember what they did with it, but it sure was fun seeing them so happy.

I thought I was so grown up when Glenda was My Mom. We both got tickled when I realized her shoes fit me. I would put them on and parade around in the house. Glenda was a very petite lady and probably wasn't even 5 feet tall. I wanted to grow up to be just like her. She was so much fun; she was always laughing. I loved her so much and loved spending time with her. When I was with Glenda, no one else existed . . . it was just her and me.

I remember my brothers getting BB guns for Christmas one year. They often shot me and my sister in the legs with them. It made me mad, but I didn't dare say anything to Dad; I knew what would happen. We also played games in the house. Vicky and I would go into the boys' room and they would turn out the lights and feel for us. They would feel for us in our private places, always on the outside of our clothes; but, obviously, they were starting to "grow up." It was always innocent play, well....as innocent as that kind of play can be.

One of my uncles gave us a tamed raccoon and we named him "Harvey." We would put Harvey on a leash and would take him everywhere with us. Harvey loved going to the baseball park. He would sit on the bleachers and watch the boys play baseball. Harvey had his own chair at the table and would eat dinner with us. He would even wash his hands before dinner. We loved Harvey; he was just like one of us kids. One day we had to leave Harvey at home when we went off for the day. Harvey didn't like being left in the garage so he got out from underneath the door and went into the back yard. Although the dogs had played with Harvey in the past, this time something went very wrong and they killed Harvey. I remember us sobbing and sobbing, "Harvey, H-A-R-V-E-Y!" It was pitiful. My dad thought it rather comical, us carrying on so about an animal. You would have thought we lost a brother or sister, not a pet raccoon.

My stepbrother Larry loved playing baseball and was the team pitcher. Dad pushed him to excel at it and that he did. In Larry's older years, he was drafted to play with the Atlanta Braves. However, Larry and three other drafted players were on their way to spring training when they were all killed in a head-on collision.

One year I was chosen to represent Larry's team as team princess. Only one girl out of the league would win the title "Small Fry Queen." Glenda had a beautiful long dress made for me and bought me a pair of new dress shoes. I felt really special that year. Mom and I were both shedding tears when they called out my name. We both cried as they put the crown on my head and the cape around my shoulders. They gave me a princess baton and a beautiful trophy. I felt so pretty, so special and so loved that day. I think I remember my dad giving me a hug after I was crowned. Little did I know that this would be the last special moment I would have in my childhood. This would be the last special moment Mom and I would share. Shortly after this momentous occasion, life would change forever.

Shortly after I won the title of "Small Fry Queen," we went camping with Dad's youngest brother and his family. I think this was when the drinking started again. This was when the "other dad" came out to play.

Chapter 6

The other daddy was a violent daddy. The other daddy was mean, cruel and thought about no one except himself. The other daddy was evil . . . and he was a very dangerous man.

At first the other daddy only came out to play sometimes; but the more the other daddy came out to play, the more he stayed out to play. One day the other daddy refused to go back inside, and he finally completely took over the daddy I adored. I didn't like this daddy and I didn't want to be around him. This daddy terrified me and with good reason. This daddy could not be trusted and this daddy remembered where I came from and who I looked like. This daddy. . . .was an evil daddy.

It all started with "incidents," incidents that Dad would apologize to Glenda for and then beg for her forgiveness. Glenda would forgive him and cycle would play out again...and yet again. One day Glenda cooked a fabulous meal, and Dad came home drunk and threw the dinner all over the walls and ceiling of the kitchen and living room. Of course, he made us kids clean it up while he begged Glenda for forgiveness. I remember being disgusted with him, not only because of what he did but because Glenda was so nice and didn't deserve it. I couldn't understand how he could treat her like that.

Dad was a coin collector. He used to collect silver coins and special bills. One day Danny and Robby stole his entire collection and spent it. Do you think he made Danny get a job and replace the value of the collection he stole? No way! Instead, he used a "creative technique" to make a point. At dinner time, in a drunken stupor, he took Danny and Robby and stood them at the end of the table in front of the wall, arms outstretched, and pitched every knife we had at the two of them as if he were a trained knife thrower in a carnival. When Dad ran out of knives, he threw a carving fork and anything else that would stick into the wall. You could tell he was in a full rage and there was no stopping him. Danny and Robby were scared to death, their eyes wide in terror. Frozen in horror, we just sat at the table watching. To have tried to stop him would have been a very stupid and dangerous move.

I have no idea how, but somehow he missed them. Not a drop of blood was shed that day. I was a kid and I remember thinking, "Well, I'm sure that's going to teach them not to steal anymore!" I remember being extremely disgusted with my dad *again* and wondering what kind of mind could possibly pitch knives at a child for punishment. I had a hard time trying to figure that one out, and it scared me to death to think of the demented mind it would take for a person to even think of something like that.

I saw the horror in Glenda's eyes that day and I knew....I knew this wonderful childhood wasn't going to last a lifetime. I knew in that moment that our days of being mother and daughter were numbered.

Danny was not a very studious child. It wasn't his fault -- he was a product of his environment. One day after he had gotten home from work, Dad looked at Danny's report card and wasn't very pleased with what he saw. Unfortunately, Danny happened to be in the bathtub at that exact moment. Consider it a bad timing thing. Dad immediately went into the closet, cut the cord off the vacuum cleaner, went into the bathroom where Danny was bare bottomed and proceeded to tear, yes, literally tear his bottom up with that cord. WOW. Amazingly, his grades never got any better. I was thinking, "Now you're going to have to buy a new vacuum cleaner, duh . . ." I never remember anyone sitting down with Danny and teaching him anything; all I remember is beatings to scare him into better grades. I could never understand Dad's behavior modification techniques and I was just a kid.

In between the moments of trauma, there were still moments of good times with Dad. This was when he was in his Jekyll and Hyde phase. One week it was Good Dad, the next week it was Evil Dad.

One day I was in Glenda's and Dad's room where he had an instant camera sitting on the dresser. I was curious so I pushed the button and the flash went off. Dad was in the living room and saw what happened. He came storming into the bedroom and hit me in the face really, really hard. When Glenda came in to take up for me, he got even angrier. He called me names and said I was just like my mother, hit me again and put me outside on the trash pile. I don't know if I was so scared I don't remember going outside or if I was unconscious when he put me on the trash pile. All I remember is waking up outside, on the trash pile with nothing on but my panties and it was now dark. I knocked on the door and Glenda's bedroom window, but no one let me in. After a bit, I crawled into the doghouse and went to sleep. We didn't have a dog at the time, so I was all by myself. The weather was changing and, although the days were fairly nice, the nights were still rather chilly. When I woke up, I noticed I had the word "trash" on me. I can't remember if it was a sign or if the words were written on my chest. I must have been in the third or fourth grade at the time.

The next morning Glenda let me inside after Dad left for work. I think being outside made me really, really sick. A couple of nights after that, I didn't feel good and I went to Glenda while she was sleeping. I quietly tiptoed to her side of the bed, tapped her on the arm and said, "Mommy, I'm not feeling very good." She quietly got out of bed and felt my head. She suddenly got scared and woke Dad. Then she called a neighbor who came over to help. I had a really high fever but Dad wouldn't let Glenda take me to the hospital. I think he was afraid they would admit me again. She didn't know what to do, so she called the hospital and they said to put me in a bath of ice. I remember being in cold water with lots of ice surrounding me. There was so much ice, I thought she was trying to freeze me to death. My fever came down and I was out of danger for the time being. However, the next day my fever started to spike again, but Dad still wouldn't let Glenda take me to the doctor. When Glenda's friend found out, they both took me to the doctor and Glenda's friend paid for it. The doctor gave me a couple of shots and medicine to take.

Shortly after this event, Dad took us kids shooting. He made each of us shoot one of his shotguns. I think the gun was longer than I was tall, or it seemed like it anyway. I remember not wanting to shoot it but he made me. For starters, I didn't want to be around my dad with a loaded gun; that really scared me. At this point I was terrified of him again. I no longer adored this man my father had turned into and I didn't want him teaching me anything, but he made me shoot the gun anyway. I'm pretty sure he had been drinking. He wasn't stupid drunk yet, but he was well on his way. I remember him putting the gun up to my shoulder. It was too heavy and big for me to hold, so he had to hold it with me. I remember my finger wasn't strong enough to pull the trigger, so he put both of my hands on the trigger while he held it up to my shoulder. There was a few inches between the end of the gun and my shoulder so when I pulled the trigger, it came back and knocked me down....hard. I fell to the ground screaming and crying. As he pointed the gun at me, I remember him saying that if I didn't shut up he was going to shoot me. Needless to say, I instantly stopped crying. My shoulder was very sore and I had a terrible bruise on it for quite some time. Life was becoming scarier and scarier.

I'll never forget the day when a poor stray cat came into our backyard. My dad hated cats. All of us kids were outside in the backyard with Dad when he picked the cat up and threw it on the concrete patio. He threw the poor cat so hard, it stunned him. As the cat lay helpless on the concrete, Dad reached down and picked him up again. He threw the poor cat down on the concrete again, and again, and again. When the cat's insides were coming out of its mouth, Dad finally picked him up one last time and kicked him into the yard behind us where a large dog lived. I don't know if the dog ate it or what; I just went inside, sad about what had just happened. I felt so sorry for the poor little cat -- he just wanted someone to love him.

This was probably around the time when my sister and I stopped being kids again. Instead of playing, my sister and I had nightly dish duty. We had to pull a chair up to the sink to reach it. Yes, all kids need to do chores, but this went beyond chores. If the dishes weren't up to Dad's standards, he would hit us with the offending plate or pan. Once he jabbed us with a fork. On Saturdays and Sundays we would spend the entire weekend helping Glenda clean house. We cleaned house from one end to the other. It was often an all-day task and Dad was never happy with the results. Dad must have been on Glenda pretty hard for her to make us clean for what seemed most of our free time. Dad was just as hard on Glenda as he was with us girls. If the house wasn't up to his standards, he would throw a major tantrum . . . and it was never up to his standards. There was no more television shows for us and no more music playing in the background. Gone was the childhood we craved for so long and had for such a little while. How could he do this to us again?

There was one day I will never forget. It was a beautiful sunny summer day; the windows and front door were open. I have no idea what the argument was about, but Dad was drunk and Glenda and Dad were really going at it. I remember it was on a weekend day, my sister and I were at the sofa folding a load of laundry. Dad got his shotgun out of the closet and loaded it. Then he backed Glenda up against the washing machine in the kitchen with the gun. Dad's next move was to put the loaded shotgun to Glenda's head. I was crying and screaming pleading with him to please stop. I was too hysterical to realize just how dangerous the situation was. The other kids knew better than to say anything. They knew if Dad would listen to anyone, it would be me. We were terrified and all of us were crying. I was still begging him to put the gun down when he suddenly turned the gun on me and shot. A teenage family friend who happened to be in the house grabbed me and threw me out the window. Thank goodness there was no screen on the window! The gunshot made a huge hole in the carpet and floor. If I had been standing there and the gun shot didn't kill me, it would surely have maimed me for life. It was a VERY close shot. Since I was only about 8 or 9 at the time and small for my age, at the very least it would have taken both my legs completely off. My dad never showed ANY remorse for that. He never apologized. Nothing. He just acted as if it never happened. I could never understand that. I was beyond disgusted with him at that point.

When the police came, Dad said he was cleaning his gun and it went off. They believed him, and they left. He knew how to manipulate the situation and he knew he could get away with murder; after all, he was experienced at it. Us kids, we knew better than to say anything different; we just agreed with what he told them. Glenda knew she had better not say anything different either. I think Glenda *knew* that had he not fired that shot at me, more than likely, it would have been fired at her. He had the devil in his eyes that day. I would come to know that look all too well. When a man has that look in his eyes, you do everything they say, just the way they say to do it and be glad you wake up the next morning. Yes, Glenda was a very lucky woman that day, and I think she knew it.

The first chance Glenda got after that, she took her luck, her boys, and even her step kids and left. Glenda loved us . . . she loved us as her very own. Her entire family did. Dad was a very lucky man to have found a woman like her. Glenda moved us to a single-wide mobile home someplace in Tennessee. I remember going to school there for a little while. During that time while we lived in Tennessee, back in South Carolina, Dad had passed out with a cigarette in his hand and burned our house down. A passerby pulled him from the fire. Yes, he survived. After that, Dad came to Tennessee and got his kids and made us go back home. It had been two or three months, maybe even more. He tried to get Glenda to go back with us telling her that he had the master bedroom painted her favorite color, lavender. And of course the same ole, same ole.... you know: "It'll be different; I was having a hard time; I didn't mean to and it will never happen again"; the typical lines. Yeah . . . right. She knew better than to go back; she knew her life depended on her staying in Tennessee. He figured if he took his kids that she would go back for our sake, but that didn't work either. She knew her life depended on her staying away from him. I missed her terribly, but I knew she had to stay away......if she wanted to live.

Chapter 7

Life without My Mom was no life for a child, especially a child like me. How would I survive without the one person I had come to truly love and adore, the one person I knew I could trust and who loved me so much? How was I supposed to live without my mother?

Life at home wasn't the same without Glenda there. Dad wasn't around much and when he was, it wasn't pretty. So we preferred for him to stay gone. When children are left alone for hours at a time and sometimes days at a time, it's never a good thing. We cooked for ourselves and we got ourselves off to school each morning. We tried to exist as adults, but we were merely kids pretending to be adults.

One day when Dad was home, he took us on a fire rescue call. A boy had drowned and Dad went to help with the rescue of the body. Dad took us with him but made us stay in the car. Although we were in the car, we saw the boy's body as they fished it from the lake. I thought it rather odd that his arms and legs were contorted in weird positions. It looked as if he were a posed statue and he looked to be as hard as one. I didn't know dead bodies could be stuck in other positions besides laying down flat. The vision of his contorted body under the white sheet haunted me for a very long time. I started wondering if my mother's body was all misshapened like his was when she died. I don't think *any* adult in their right mind would have taken kids to something like that. I remember some of the guys pointing to us in the car, and I think they were questioning Dad's decision to bring us along. I do know this was his last rescue mission.

Dad was drinking more and becoming more violent. He started taking me with him when he went to his favorite bar. I don't really remember what prompted that. I probably asked to go; I enjoyed staying busy and going anywhere. Dad was a frequent visitor and everyone knew him, so they welcomed me with open arms. Dad would play Elvis' "Hunk of Burnin Love" on the Juke Box, and I would dance up a storm. I always had an ear for music and I loved it. It got to be quite the show: I would go with him, dance up a storm, the other patrons would get up and dance, and Dad would get more free beer. Dad once said he was going to "make a killing" off of me one day. The patrons would get tickled at the way I could move for such a little girl. Dad said I was his "little dancer" and that I was going to make a lot of money for him. Dad would always say to everyone, "This one, this one here…. she's my pride and joy." When he got extremely drunk he would often call me Diane, my mother's name. I looked a lot like her when I was that age. I was flattered Dad was saying such wonderful things about me. He made me feel loved and wanted when he talked about me so. I remember thinking, "Wow, he does love me!" In a normal family setting, this would be far from love. It's rather obvious that my perception of love was rather distorted.

One day Danny got into some of Dad's 8mm films, films that were not meant for children to see. I went into Dad's room where Danny was, and we started watching Dad's movies. I didn't think anything of it at the time … I had no idea what they were or that they weren't intended for children. No one had ever spoken to us about our bodies, about life or sex. To us this was just a natural progression. We weren't taught right from wrong except in daily life when it would upset my Dad … when he was around, that is. But sex, drugs, stealing from stores, boundaries with our bodies -- everything children should have known by then -- was either not taught to us, or taught erratically. There was absolutely no consistency about the things taught or the way they were taught.

Danny thought it would be fun to replicate what we were watching and I was adventurous enough to say "Sure." I thought "O.K. That's what grownups do," so I thought this was okay for us to do, too. After all, we were taking care of ourselves and were now adults. I must have been around 9 or 10 at the time. What we were watching was something children should never be watching and it definitely wasn't something children should be trying to replicate. Although at the time I had no idea what was going on, Danny tried to have sex with me. We were just following the movie. When I told Danny to stop, he didn't force himself on me but stopped as I asked. I told him I didn't want to do that anymore, so I put my clothes on, ate my dinner and went over to play with Kathie. It wasn't anything anyone had told me was something we shouldn't be doing, but I was beginning to feel uneasy at my house. After this, I started spending more time next door with my friend Kathie.

Kathie had Cerebral Palsy and had to spend most of her time indoors. I spent a lot of time at her house entertaining her, and we had become best friends. Kathie was older than me. She must have been about sixteen at the time. Even though no one had explained life to me, somehow I knew a lot of bad stuff was happening at my house and I didn't want to be there. So I spent most of my days and even most of my nights at Kathie's house. Kathie was so sweet and we loved spending time with each other. She tried to teach me how to knit. I wasn't very good at it, but I kept trying anyway. Kathie and I watched TV together; that was what we did most. By this time most of my other friends were no longer allowed to play with me, so Kathie was pretty much my only friend. Parents don't let their children play with children like us.

There was a lady a few houses down from us who took an interest in me. She would give me a couple of dollars to watch her toddler while she cleaned house. She talked to me about God and invited me to church several times. During the summer my sister and I rode the church bus to vacation bible school. This was the first time I had ever heard about God and Jesus. I remember being so confused as to whether he was God or if he was Jesus. I just figured some people called this man God and that Jesus was his nickname. I was baptized during vacation bible school, mainly because I could tell it would make everyone at church happy and that was what they wanted me to do. One Sunday after I was baptized, my dad came to church. During the invitation, Dad went to the front of the church. He cried and made quite a scene. I found this all very embarrassing and I was disgusted with him for doing what he did. I had seen him promise words to women for years, but he never kept his word and I knew he didn't mean anything he said this time. He was merely spewing words to make people feel sorry for him, but he had no intentions of changing. The men and women in the church thought, "Oh, look! He's going to change his ways." But I knew better. A couple of weeks later Dad wouldn't let us go to church anymore. I think maybe he was embarrassed by his actions. He said we were only going to church so we wouldn't have to clean house. We were only allowed to attend church for about six weeks, but it was long enough for me to know I had another Father and that this Father loved me.

I continued to spend more and more time at Kathie's house and very little time at my house. I had a bed in Kathie's room and I became part of their family. I didn't see Danny or my sister often, but I knew things were pretty bad over there. Dad once scared me when he came home and started calling me Diane as he tried hugging me more than a father should hug a daughter and started touching me all over. So I knew that wasn't a place for me to be, especially at night. I heard conversations about taking food from the store and other things, so I know Dad wasn't providing much. I'm sure I spent some time there, but I don't really remember it. For the most part, I lived next door at Kathie's; and I made sure I was never at my house at night time when I knew Dad would be there.

Sometime before Easter that year, my dad gave Ms. Kendall -- Kathie's mother -- money and asked her to take my sister and me shopping for a new Easter outfit. We went to the store to the big girl section and found the cutest little pink and cream pantsuit for my sister. I thought it was really pretty; it looked like an outfit that grown women would wear. It was dressy and feminine, something I would have liked for myself. It had a wrap style print top and the slacks were all pink. I was hoping we could find something that sophisticated and beautiful for me. Then we went over to the little girl department to find something for me. I wound up with a pair of hideous red, white, and blue pants with a wide navy blue elastic waist band and a navy blue top. There was nothing feminine or dressy about it; but Ms. Kendall was having a hard time finding something that fit me, much less something I liked that fit. So, needless to say, I was pretty melancholy that day. We both got a new pair of socks and new panties as well. Then Ms. Kendall took Vicky to the lingerie department and bought her a bra, a bra with actual cups. Well, I decided right then and there that I wasn't going to leave that department without one for me, too. Ms. Kendall said to me, "But, Sweetie, you don't need a bra. You don't have any bosoms yet." Adamantly, I told her I needed a training bra, I thought I didn't have bosoms because I hadn't been training them. I was *seriously* terrified that if I didn't get a bra that day, I would never ever have breasts. I was almost hysterical about the situation, crying and having such a fit. I kept trying to make Mrs. Kendall understand that and that if I didn't get a training bra *that day*, I would never have any breasts. Needless to say, no one had talked to us about the facts of life and what to expect from our bodies as they matured. I finally convinced her I needed one, and so she bought me my first training bra. I felt so grown. I saw her laughing, and I couldn't figure out why she thought this whole ordeal was so funny. In fact, as I looked around, I noticed several women were chuckling over it. I thought it was serious business, and there they were laughing at me!

I was so proud. I couldn't wear big girl clothes yet; but, hey, that was okay because I was finally going to have breasts. I couldn't wait to get home and put on my bra so I could start training them to grow. I would check them every day to see if they had started growing yet. I wondered how long the training process would take before I saw results. After a few days of nothing, I started sleeping in it and every morning I would check the results again. Since they weren't growing yet, I thought if I wore it all the time, they would finally start growing. You know what? It didn't work. But I still wore my bra all the time, just in case. A few months later when Social Services came to school and pulled me from class to ask me questions about my dad, it was in my pocket. I had worn it so much it had broken. You know, for some reason, that bra must have been defective because it wasn't working. But, honestly, I think it was because God was looking out for me. It would come to be that not having my budding breasts yet would be a blessing.

We didn't know what that shopping trip was all about, and we knew better than to question anything. But it was nice to just enjoy a shopping trip. This was our first shopping trip since Glenda had left Dad; and since he had never taken us shopping before, we were definitely in need of some new things. Dad was a man who didn't part easily with his money and we often went without.

Glenda had been gone for quite some time when, out of the blue, my father told us to put on our nice outfits and get in the car. We were now around 10, 11 & 12. We didn't know where we were going. We merely got dressed and did as we were told. With violent alcoholics, YOU NEVER QUESTION ANYTHING -- you merely do as you're told. So off we headed down the road, and after awhile we realized we were on our way to Tennessee. We weren't prepared for a trip from Charleston, South Carolina, to Knoxville, Tennessee; we only had the clothes we were wearing and nothing else.

On the way to Tennessee, Dad stopped to gas up the car. When he paid for the gas, I noticed they had little dyed baby chicks on sale. I begged and begged and Dad finally gave in and bought one for me. I was so tickled. Here I was in my training bra, training my bosoms like a real lady; and today I was a momma. I was a momma to a baby chick. I was going to take care of that chick forever. I felt like the mother of a newborn baby. This was the first living thing that I had ever owned and it was all mine. I could tell it already loved me and I loved it. I fed and gave it water all the way to Tennessee. We curled up and napped together, and I fed it some more and gave it more water. I vowed to be the best momma ever. This chick and I, we were a family, my own little family; and we loved each other so much.

I was very excited about our trip; I missed Glenda so much. She was the only mother I'd ever known. She was going to be excited about my chick and proud of my mothering abilities. Something I loved that loved me back. Being a new momma felt so incredible. We were driving and I could already see the smile on her face. She was going to be so proud of me. Glenda was going to be so proud to see I've grown up so much and was now a woman and a momma.

50

The closer we got to Tennessee, the drunker my dad got; and the closer we got, the colder it got. We were driving through the Tennessee mountains, and there was snow on the road. Even worse, there was ice. We were scared to death! As the car weaved and skidded from side to side, we held on and peered with alarm down the side of the mountain each time we slid dangerously close to the road's edge. As we swerved, we gripped the arm rests tighter and tighter in silence, too afraid to even make a sound. At one point Dad almost drove off the side of the mountain, but he swerved and slammed against the mountain wall on the other side of the road. As my dad got out of the car to assess the damage, another car stopped and a man got out. I felt so relieved to see someone helping my dad. I thought we were finally safe, but Dad told him everything was fine and he sent him away. As Dad staggered back to our car and the man got back into his car, he looked at us. You could see the pain and anger in his face as he peered into three sets of terrified little eyes. I remember staring directly into this man's eyes as if to say, "Help me, please help me, Mister! Please don't let him take us." You could tell by the look on his face that he was very afraid for our lives that day. I watched as he sat banging on his steering wheel in helplessness, afraid we would never make it to our destination and knowing there was nothing he could do to stop it. Although I was very scared while Dad was swerving while driving up the mountain, after looking at this man's reactions, I suddenly became terrified. He had just confirmed my worst fears.

As Dad pulled away from the car, the man just sat there, quietly watching. I watched the man's car as we rounded the next curve and could no longer see it anymore. A deep dark sadness set in and during the rest of the trip I just sat quietly, concentrating on my precious little baby bird. I truly did not think we would be alive much longer, and I didn't want to be looking out the window when our car drove off the side of the mountain. So I just concentrated as hard as I could on my little baby bird, trying to keep my mind off of our impending death. This bird was all I really had. I FINALLY had something that loved me. I was talking to God and telling him how I was going to be the kind of mother to this bird that I never had, that I was going to take care of it and love it. He was really hungry, and -- being such a wonderful mommy -- I kept feeding him like good mommies do.

I was so proud of myself and I smiled, knowing that God must have been proud of me, too.

Somehow, we made it to our destination that day. Dad had driven us to Glenda's brother's house, but no one was there. So, he decided to just drop us off. He dropped us off in the woods close to their home and headed back home to South Carolina without us. There we sat, in the woods with night quickly falling -- cold, hungry and wondering what to do. It was scary. I felt so alone, unloved, unwanted and disposable. We were left all alone in the middle of the woods -- no coats, no food . . . nothing. I started crying, not silent little cries, but sobbing cries. As I sat there sobbing and petting my bird, I was thinking this bird was the only thing that loved me. Then all of a sudden, his belly burst open; and all the food I had fed him started rolling out. My precious little baby bird had just died in my hands. That was it! That was all I could handle. I started sobbing even harder, and I was so angry. It felt as if a real baby had just died in my hands....*my* baby. The only thing in this world that loved me, just died in my hands. I was devastated. My brother came over, grabbed the bird and threw it as far as he could throw it. I fell to my knees, put my face into my hands and just sobbed. I didn't know what else to do. I was so angry at God, that in my mind I started yelling at him. I was on my knees in the middle of the woods with my face in my hands, sobbing and yelling at God. I was asking God, "WHY? WHY DO YOU HATE ME SO MUCH? WHY DO YOU HATE ME SO MUCH THAT YOU GAVE ME A LIFE LIKE THIS? WHAT HAVE I DONE TO CAUSE YOU TO HATE ME SO MUCH? I'M JUST A LITTLE GIRL -- I DON'T UNDERSTAND. I TRY SO HARD TO BE SO GOOD AND I JUST DON'T UNDERSTAND! I MAKE GOOD GRADES; I DO EVERYTHING I'M TOLD AND I NEVER TALK SO I DON'T SAY ANYTHING WRONG." I told God, "NO CHILD DESERVES A LIFE LIKE THIS. I'M JUST A LITTLE GIRL, AND I JUST CAN'T UNDERSTAND WHY YOU HATE ME SOOOOO MUCH." God didn't answer me that day.

That day felt like the loneliest day of my life. I wondered then, being all of 9 or 10, why? Why did so much bad stuff happen to us? Nobody loved me; nobody wanted me; I didn't even feel like a woman in bloom any more. I felt crippled and helpless, unloved and unwanted. I just couldn't understand why. I had been so good. I made A's in school; I was talking much better and stuttered a lot less. I was talking to God and asking him, "What did I do? Why can't someone --*anyone* -- just love me? What is so bad about me that I am so unlovable?" The sobbing had settled down, but I continued my conversation with God. I told Him that no matter what he had put in front of me, I thought I had handled it in an okay kind of way. I always smiled and was still caring and loving even with all the hurt and pain in my life. And since I had a really big heart, the hurt never stayed very long. It would go away rather quickly and I would be happy and smiles again. I couldn't understand what I had done so bad that I deserved all of this pain. I was as broken as a person could get -- and I was just a little girl. I was tired of so much pain. There were good moments, too, but there was so much pain. All I wanted was to be loved and cared for. I didn't think I was asking for too much. We had a rather long chat. I was so engrossed in my quiet conversation with God, crying the whole time, that I didn't notice or hear Danny break the glass window of the house. Since it was night and close to freezing, he broke a window so we could get out of the cold and get some food. It was really cold outside at night in spring in the Tennessee mountains. Once inside, we helped ourselves to food and covers and went to bed. No one showed up that night. There we were, three little kids taking care of ourselves, yet again. Being physically, mentally and emotionally exhausted, I didn't have any trouble getting to sleep that night. I had nothing more to give, and it was all I could do to make it to bed.

The next morning Glenda's family came home to find three little kids asleep in their beds. I was so happy to see Glenda; it was almost like a fairy tale. Life was miserable when I went to sleep, and I woke up safe in My Mommy's arms. I wanted to stay in those wonderful arms forever. Glenda held me for a long time and cried with me. She seemed so sad. I couldn't understand why she was so, so sad; but it felt so good to be in her arms. It felt so good to have her hold me and hug me again. I was thinking that, hopefully, since she wanted to see us, maybe I could talk her into letting me stay. I wanted to stay some place for a little while that wasn't so painful. My life was too painful; I couldn't take anymore. I didn't want to go back "there." I was too tired. I was emotionally and mentally exhausted. I needed a break. I needed to be loved for just a little while. I loved being with Glenda -- she was My Mommy. We played for awhile and life was so good. I think I was still crying, but I was also enjoying time with her and just reveling in it. I loved her so much. Thinking back on it, I was so emotionally broken that I literally had nothing more to give. I was in a very scary state of mind, and I was just a little girl.

We played the rest of the day, and I think I even stopped crying later that afternoon. I remember Glenda tucking us in that night, and I couldn't wait to see her the next morning. The next morning, I awoke and we ate breakfast and played. After a little while, Glenda asked me to come sit on her lap. I was all smiles as I skipped over to her and sat in her lap. Then she wrapped her arms around me and told me my dad was there to pick me up. She was crying when she told me. You could tell she didn't want to send us back . . . but she knew her life depended on it. When she told me Dad was there to pick me up, I started screaming and crying. I was begging her, "MOMMY, PLEASE DON'T MAKE ME GO! PLEASE LET ME STAY! PLEASE DON'T MAKE ME GO. I PROMISE I'LL BE REALLY GOOD. PLEASE, OH PLEASE, DON'T MAKE ME GO! PLEASE, MOMMY, PLEASE LET ME STAY WITH YOU. DON'T MAKE ME GO WITH HIM!" They had to tear me out of her arms that day to put me back in the car with *THAT MAN*. That was the last time I ever saw Glenda, and that was the time my heart died.

I tried to put my arms and legs out so they couldn't get me in the car, but Dad yelled at me and I knew to be quiet and do as I was told. He was so drunk that he couldn't even sit up. He was lying in the back seat of my uncle's station wagon and was slurring every word out of his evil, foul mouth. I climbed over him and got into the back compartment. Dad had a younger brother who was just as mean as he was, if not meaner, and *he* drove us home that day.

Later down the mountain, Dad hollered, "Helen, come here, come sit with your daddy." I did as I was told. The next thing I knew, he reached up and put his hand under my shirt and said, "Oh heck, you don't have anything!" Then he gruffly told me to go get in the back of the car. I did as I was told. I think I knew what was going on, what he wanted from me; but all I could think about was how grateful I was to "not have anything." At first I felt insulted, but that was quickly replaced with gratefulness. Ironically, three weeks earlier, I was trying desperately to get a training bra because I was seriously afraid I would never have any bosoms; but now I was so thankful I didn't have any. Then Dad hollered for my sister. All I could think was, *"I'm so glad that's not me."* I didn't feel sorry for my sister at all. All I could allow myself to think was, *"I am so glad that isn't me."* I felt bad because I didn't want it to be me; and, therefore, it had to be her. I felt so bad inside for thinking that, but I couldn't do anything about it. All I could do was to survive myself. It took every ounce of energy I had in me to merely survive myself. I had nothing else to give….nothing. I truly felt lifeless and dead inside. Something horrible happened inside when they pulled me out of Glenda's arms. I couldn't put my finger on it, but life would never be the same. There was an intense darkness that consumed every fiber of my being at that moment, and I truly felt as if I were dead inside.

After we made it back to South Carolina, I immediately went to visit my friend, Kathie, next door. Kathie was my safe place. When I was there, I was safe. I spent A LOT of time with Kathie. I visited with her and cried all that day. She tried everything she could to console me, but all I could do was cry. My life was such a mess. Kathie had saved part of her chocolate Easter bunny for me; and as I ate my chocolate, I was still crying. I was so broken and so devastated that nothing could console me -- not even chocolate! My dad came over to get me to take me home, but Kathie's mom said, "Look at her, Leroy! She can't take anymore. Look at this child. *She cannot take ANYMORE!!* Let her stay here with us." Finally, he agreed. I never even looked up. I was so disgusted with him; I didn't even want to look at his evil, pathetic face. I stayed the night with Kathie and when I went to bed, I was still crying. I couldn't stop the tears. Kathie said, "Come here, Helen. Come sleep with me." I went to Kathie's bed and she held me in her arms and I finally cried myself to sleep. That was the first time I ever remember anyone holding me like that. This wonderful, sweet, crippled little girl gave me something no one else had ever given me – she loved me unconditionally. It felt so good. The next morning I awoke and I was still crying. I was a 10 year old girl, and I couldn't take ANY more. I couldn't take any more of my life -- and I was only 10 years old. I was completely emotionally and mentally broken and exhausted. I was as close to a mental breakdown as a person could get, and I was a 10 year old *child*. I truly think if I had gone home that night and one more emotional thing happened, I would not be sitting here writing my story. I was seriously on the brink of a complete and total mental breakdown. I truly feel that if I had gone home that day, I would probably be living in an insane asylum today. I was teetering on the edge of insanity at that time in my life.

The next night Dad came over. He wanted me to run down the road to a neighbor's house to pick up a pair of pants they were hemming for him. I loved to run, so I didn't mind. It was dark outside, and I didn't see the broken bottle as I stepped on it with my bare feet. The bottle cut my foot really badly and I had to hop back. When I got back to Kathie's house, blood was pouring from my foot. Kathie's mother told Dad I needed stitches. I remember Dad saying, "Heck, no! Just bandage it up and she'll be fine." After Ms. Kendall argued with Dad some more, she realized there was no other choice but to stop the bleeding and bandage it up.

Dad went down to get his own pants, and then he went out on the town to party. I stayed on Kathie's sofa and off my badly cut foot.

THE FOSTER YEARS

"Smile despite the circumstances
and laugh throughout the pain.
Life is full of hardships,
but it is how you deal with them
that will, in the end,
define you."

Chapter 8

The next day there was a knock at the door. Kathie's mom answered it and it was my sister, Vicky; she wanted me to come to the door. Ms. Kendall asked Vicky to come in to talk to me because of my foot, but Vicky wanted me to come to the door instead. Ms. Kendall was a little irritated but said the door was for me, so I hobbled to the door to see who it was. Suddenly, chaos erupted yet again. Here I am in my safe place; and the next thing you know, two hands broke through the screen door and pulled me through it. A man and my sister ran me down to a car, threw me in and took off. My aunt who lived nearby was driving so I knew it was safe; but, of course, I had no idea what was going on or where we were going. The three of us kids were driven to the Department of Family and Children Services (DFCS) where my aunt left us. We spent several hours answering questions at the DFCS office. They didn't question me much -- they just kept me in one spot with my leg propped up. They were concerned about my foot and had someone look at it to see if it needed immediate attention.

After spending most of the day at the DFCS office, they decided to take the three of us to a youth detention center. They felt so certain that our father would kill us for telling the truth that they kept us locked up for what seemed several months. They locked us up to protect us from our own father! They had to lock me up to *SAVE* me from the one person who was supposed to love and protect me.

I was all of ten years old, and I will never forget that they made me strip down like a common criminal and bathe while a stranger watched me. They checked all of my orifices and then gave me a set of clothes to put on that they typically give children who are criminals. They had a hard time trying to find anything to fit, so we had to improvise a little. I remember them having to tie the belt loops together on the pants to make them small enough to stay up. I asked for a bra and someone said "Oh, you don't need one yet." I immediately let them know that I had already started wearing a bra. So, after some hesitation and much discussion, they gave me one anyway. I thought it was awesome. This bra had real cups in it. I thought I felt like a much older person now, a full grown woman. I never gave much thought about not having any bosoms to fill the cups. The important thing to me at the time was that it *looked* as if I had real bosoms. I remember a discussion about letting me sleep in the infirmary, although I had no idea what an infirmary was. I just remember them being concerned with me not sleeping in the same room as my sister and being locked in a jail room all by myself. They decided against me sleeping in the infirmary and locked me in a room, by myself, like a common criminal.

The first night they locked me in, I cried. It reminded me of the closet we used to live in. In time, I got used to it and actually enjoyed being by myself. I loved my sister but thought she could be rather controlling and pretty mean to me. So, I enjoyed just being by myself in my own room where I could do anything I wanted and not worry about making anyone angry.

Dad showed up at the juvenile detention center and became belligerent and violent. I remember several men grabbing his arms. I think maybe they were arresting him. I watched him from the corner of my eye because I was too afraid to look at him. I was afraid that if he saw me looking at him, acknowledging he was there, that I would get in trouble because I didn't go to him. I didn't realize at the time that there was no way I could get out of the room where I was even if I wanted to. Thinking back on it now, I do think they were arresting my dad. I was sitting at a table, building with cards, pretending to ignore the chaos, yet watching what was going on with him. I felt safe because I was behind a thick wall of glass. This was the last time I remember seeing my dad during my childhood.

I'll never forget living at the detention center. It was a very different type of life. We weren't free to roam; we couldn't go outside whenever we wanted to; there was no play time; our life was not our own; and, to be honest, it was pretty boring. We were subjected to all the rules the criminal children had to abide by. One day when we were put in line for showers, they had us buddy up with a partner. There were quite a few kids in the juvenile detention center at the time, and we only had so much time to allow for showers. There was a girl there who was of color and I shouted and said, "I want to get a shower with her," as I pointed to her. In my mind I was wondering if her female areas where of color or white like ours. Without any words passed, she knew immediately what I was curious about and called me out on it. She informed me that *ALL* of her body parts were the same color as her skin. Well, she actually said it a little differently, but I won't repeat her exact words. I was so embarrassed. I was shocked that she knew what I was thinking. Her angry reaction and very sharp teeth terrified me. Needless to say, they made me take a shower with my sister instead.

A couple of days after living at the youth detention center, our case worker, Mr. Cox, came to take me to the doctor to have my foot examined. The doctor and he said the wound should have been stitched up but that it was now too late for stitches. They talked about reopening and suturing it so it would be a much cleaner scar, but decided against it. Instead, they gave me a solution to soak it in for the infection, a shot and antibiotics. Mr. Cox took me out for lunch that day. That was the first time I ever remember going to a real restaurant. I thought it was pretty awesome. I also thought Mr. Cox was kind of cute and fun, and I enjoyed spending time with him.

This whole time, all I had been doing was hopping around the center on one foot. I couldn't walk on my foot or put any pressure on it, so the doctor gave me a pair of crutches. At first I thought it was cool, but it didn't take very long before my underarms got really sore from using them and I wanted to go back to hopping around. The center wouldn't let me hop around anymore. Eventually, I got used to the crutches and my foot got better quickly.

We were in juvenile detention for so long that we had to attend school there. We weren't allowed to leave the building for school; instead, they had their own teachers. I enjoyed going to school there because we were able to work at our own speed. I enjoyed learning and it came easy for me. In this environment, I was able to work beyond my grade. I was excited about being challenged academically. I learned that if I studied hard enough, I didn't have time for the bad memories to take over. The more effort I put into school, the less time I had for looking back or for the bad memories to flood my mind. So, I slowly replaced the bad memories with academic challenge.

After several months of living in the detention center, I was given my old clothes and was told to get dressed because we had a court date. My old clothes barely fit and I only had one shoe. Nobody explained what court was or what was going to be taking place there, but I did as I was told, as always. My foot was doing better now and I was wearing two shoes in the center. However, when I was thrown into the car, I only had the clothes I was wearing when I arrived; therefore, I only had one shoe. Rather than walking into court with one shoe, I hopped on one foot acting as if I still couldn't use my hurt foot. I was too embarrassed by the situation to let anyone know I only had one shoe. I couldn't understand why the center wouldn't let me wear a pair of their shoes as I didn't realize we wouldn't be returning.

I was expecting to see Dad at court, but he wasn't there. After court we didn't go back to the juvenile detention center; instead, we went to our first foster home. Again, no one explained where we were going or what was about to take place. We were just dropped off and left at a stranger's house. We were dropped off at the house of Sam and Sue Wagener. I remember when Sam and Sue opened their door that Sam had long hair, a long beard and a moustache. Sue had really long wavy hair, a beautiful smile and she was obviously pregnant. Sam and Sue invited us into their house and seemed like very happy and jolly people. They had three daughters. The oldest was Sue's biological daughter, Lori; the middle daughter was Sam's biological daughter, Patty; and the youngest, Ann, was Sue's adopted daughter. She was my age.

You could tell Sam and Sue were very smart and highly educated people. That was pretty obvious by their actions and words. I enjoyed that about them right away and could tell they would challenge me academically. Sam was a geologist and Sue was a biologist. I remember Sue saying she also tutored college students in her spare time. I wasn't sure what college was, but I could tell it was a good thing by the way she said it.

Life with the Wagener's was very different from what we were used to. Sue made everything from scratch. They ate a lot of natural foods and made us drink milk with every meal. We weren't used to milk; it was too expensive for us to buy. This took some getting used to, but I knew it was good for me.

I noticed they had a piano in one of the rooms, and I loved it. I loved any kind of music. I found it very soothing. Sam said that if I taught myself the basics, he would let me take lessons with Ann's piano teacher. I quickly taught myself how to play and Sam made good on his promise.

One of my favorite things to do was to play chess with Sam. I don't remember him letting me win -- he challenged me and I really liked that . . . or maybe he was very good at letting me think he was challenging me. Either way, I liked it. Sue had a lot to do and didn't pay much attention to me. To me it seemed as if she didn't pay *any* attention to me. I often wondered if she even liked me. I knew Sam liked me. He took time with me and frequently played chess with me; he also complimented my game. I thought that was pretty cool, especially since I had never played chess before. I really liked Sam and it seemed like Sam liked me, too. I was even starting to talk a little, and I don't remember stuttering as much. I felt calm inside; this was a very new feeling for me and I liked it. However, with all of the free time, bad memories started flooding my mind. I started thinking about my dad and was starting to miss him. Although my dad was mean and I finally felt safe there, the unknown was intensely uncomfortable and I didn't know how to deal with it. No one was telling me anything. Am I going to go back home? How long was this going to be for? What is going to happen tomorrow? Will I live here forever? How comfortable do I get? Do I allow myself to like these people, or will I be going home soon? When would I get to see Kathie and tell her about my adventure? What am I supposed to do to keep them happy? Will they change like my dad did? What exactly is a foster child anyway? There were so many questions in my head, but no one ever asked me about them or asked how I felt or what I thought. I found this uncomfortable, and it grew more and more intense every day. I wanted to go home where I knew my surroundings and where every day wasn't a mass of questions about tomorrow, where the unknown didn't haunt me every minute of every day.

Sam and Sue didn't watch television and didn't have one in their house. This took some adjusting to because we spent a lot of time watching television in our "other life." Sue spent lot of time with my sister to help her catch up in school. She was really good for my sister, and I was happy my sister was getting the attention she needed. My brother Danny was there for just a short while. I don't know where he went, just that he wasn't there for very long. I remember hearing a story about my dad. He wasn't at the court hearing because he was still in the hospital. From what I could gather, after the juvenile detention center sent my father away, he loaded his gun into the car and headed for Tennessee. Dad was planning to shoot and kill Glenda because we were taken away from him. In Dad's eyes, we were taken away from him because she had left. He never saw that he was responsible for the situation. Apparently, once Dad got to Tennessee, as he was pulling the shotgun out of the back seat, it went off and shot him in the groin.

I heard them say it was a pretty bad injury and that he was lucky to be alive. I believe I remember them saying that he almost bled to death because it either hit an artery or almost hit an artery. Either way, it concerned me and I started thinking about him more. I think this was when I started missing him. I don't know if I was missing him, or if I was missing my old life . . . . not the abusive part, but the familiar part. I was painfully shy and living in a home where I didn't know anyone. Life there was completely different from what I knew, and it was extremely hard for a child like me to adjust to it. No one seemed to notice how much I was struggling with my surroundings. No one ever talked to me about anything; I felt like a chess piece being moved around without any preparation. I never knew from one day to the next what was in store for me. No one ever asked my opinion or how I felt about anything. It was as if no one cared how I felt or what I thought. It seemed as if they thought, because I was a child, that I had absolutely no rights and didn't need to be consulted or informed about anything concerning my life. I couldn't understand how other people could make decisions that were right for me if they didn't know anything about me or who I was. I didn't like the situation I was in, and no one cared to know how I felt about it. This home was not the right fit for me, and it was starting to cause me to feel extremely uncomfortable.

All of the kids in the Wagener house attended private Catholic school. I actually enjoyed the Catholic school and enjoyed spending time with the sisters. By this time I was a baptized Baptist living with a Jewish couple and attending Catholic school. I figured I had all of the religions covered. When I started school there, they advanced me one grade higher. This meant I was now one grade above my sister. I skipped the 6th grade and went directly into the 7th grade. I really liked our uniforms, they were cute little skirts and white shirts. I liked wearing skirts -- they made me feel like a lady. I remember being a little girl who always wanted to be a woman. What I didn't like was my gold socks and my red shoes. I didn't think they matched my outfit very well, but I never told anyone. We were all assigned a different color of socks because it made laundry day much easier. I got the most hideous color. Yuk! No one ever asked me about what socks I wanted or anything else. It was getting rather annoying.

A couple of months after we moved to live with the Wagener's, I called my dad to come and get me. Although he scared me, I was hoping that he would be back to the good daddy, the daddy I adored. I wanted to go back to the familiar life I knew, back to Kathie's house. I couldn't handle the unfamiliarity of my new life the way people tossed me around and made decisions in my life without my knowledge. I never knew what was going to happen next and I found that VERY scary. At the time I thought that even being with the evil daddy who disgusted me was better than the unknown, the unfamiliar. Even though it was a horrible life, it was the only life I knew and I typically knew what was going to happen, even if it was bad stuff. I told my sister about my plans for Dad to pick me up so she could come with us. The plan was for me to take Teal, their dog, on our usual daily walk and Dad would meet me at the corner and pick me up. We would drop Teal out of the car at his house and speed away. At first she seemed excited; but right before it was to happen, she told on me. I remember Sam being pretty upset with me. That was when Sam started spending a little more time with me. I forgot about my dad after Sam starting spending more time with me, and I started to feel a little more comfortable with my new surroundings. But it still felt too different from my old life.

I adored Sue's youngest daughter, Ann. We hung out with each other all the time. We played a lot together and enjoyed each other's company. We all had our own chores and earned a weekly allowance. My sister's chores were typically working with Sue; they spent a lot of time together. Ann and I often had outdoor chores. I loved being outside and enjoyed doing our chores. This was the first time I had chores that I earned money for.

I remember I liked playing in the backyard with Ann the most. We would come up with all kinds of games and had so much fun playing in the trees. But I needed more than imaginary play. I noticed there were no toys and I wanted a Barbie to play with. I never had a Barbie and I wanted one really badly. I thought Barbie was so beautiful. I remember wanting to look like Barbie and have bosoms like Barbie. I wanted a Barbie and I dreamed of playing with her and giving her a wonderful life. I knew in my mind that, when I played with her, her life would be very different from the life that was my life. She would have the life I always longed to have. Barbie would have a wonderful and beautiful imaginary life, and I dreamed of getting lost in her beautiful life.

While we were living with the Wagener's, my sister had a paper route and I would often go with her and help her throw papers. My sister was strong and I admired her for that. One day I went with her, took the allowance I had saved and bought a Barbie doll with it. I was so proud of myself because I had purchased something I wanted with my own money. When I got home with my Barbie doll, Sam and Sue made me take it back to the store and return it. They said we weren't allowed to play with toys in their house. They said in their house we had to use our imagination to play and weren't allowed to play with toys. This upset me very much. I had to leave behind life as I knew it; I had to leave behind all of my friends and family; I had to leave behind all of my belongings and now I was being told I wasn't allowed to play with toys. I didn't want to be there anymore. I needed some time to just be a little girl. I know I often wanted to be womanly; but for a little while, I just needed to play and be a little girl. I needed to have my Barbie and pretend play a wonderful magical life for her. I needed to pretend she could have the life I was never allowed to have. I needed to fill my head with wonderful, magical little girl play so it would take over all of the horrible memories locked inside. You see, when I could only use my mind to play, it was so full of bad memories that I had a hard time wading past them to get to the pretty ones. I wanted so badly to forget them, but I couldn't when I had to dig around in there for imaginary play. At least if I had a Barbie, something beautiful and tangible, it would give me a way to bypass those ugly memories because Barbie reminded me she only deserved beautiful imaginary play. No one bothered to ask why I needed her so badly, nor did anyone really care. Their rules were their rules without understanding the implications on my mental or emotional health and stability. For foster children, rules that make sense for ordinary children, don't necessarily work the same for foster children. DFCS had a responsibility to train "the family" . . . not just parents, the entire family . . . about parenting and playing with foster children *before* we came into their house.

This life was too different for me. I didn't think Sue liked me much and I couldn't adjust. I felt the only one who really cared about me was Teal, the dog. I took Teal for walks almost every day and we talked a lot. No one cared enough to ask how I felt, so I talked to Teal. I loved Teal and I trusted Teal and Teal loved me. I felt Teal was the only one who loved me.

While we lived with the Wagener's, we all went to the dentist. I think this was our very first dentist appointment ever. The dentist found a cyst inside the boney area in my sister's mouth. She had to have surgery to have it removed. Sam had a very small television put away and my sister was allowed to watch TV while she was recuperating. We all snuck in there from time to time to watch it. I got caught and got into trouble. I missed watching television. When I watched TV, it took my mind off the bad memories.

With no outlet for my internal anger, when I got mad, I would turn the iron on upstairs and set it face down on the ironing board. I remember Sue reprimanding Lori for leaving the iron on face down. She said she didn't do it, but I think Sue thought that she did and didn't want to admit it. I remember feeling a little bad for Lori, but doing it made me feel better and not quite so angry. There wasn't any other outlet for me, and no one talked to me about the things in my life that I had no control over or about the anger caused by living a life that wasn't right for me. I was very quiet and I guess no one thought they needed to pay any attention to me or ask how I felt about anything. Sue was very busy being an expectant mother and teaching my sister. This was a good placement for my sister, but it wasn't good for me. As time passed, I began turning the iron on more and more and leaving it face down on the ironing board.

All of the Wagner girls took water ballet lessons, and my sister and I were allowed to take lessons as well. I loved swimming and enjoyed the lessons. We would do ballet legs and all types of beautiful ballet moves in the water. I felt like a swan, a beautiful swan swimming in the water creating beautiful movements. One day we were all in a circle practicing for an upcoming performance when I got too close to the girl in front of me. When she kicked up for her ballet leg, she kicked my finger and broke it. We didn't know it was broken for a couple of weeks. After the swelling wouldn't go down, I went to the doctor and he said it was broken. I had to get a splint on my finger and a cast on my arm. I didn't get to participate in the performance, but I got to watch. I watched as Lori taped lights on herself along with the other older girls and did a nighttime performance. I was in awe . . . it was beautiful. I couldn't wait until I learned to do something like that.

Sue gave birth to a baby girl. That was the first time I had ever seen a newborn baby. She was so tiny. I used to sneak into Sue's bedroom and just sit and watch her sleep. We were at the table eating dinner one night and Sue asked me if I would like to hold the baby. I must have been extremely excited because, when she put the baby in my arms, she told me I could walk into the other room with her. Later that night Ann told me Sue did that because as soon as I left the room she started crying. Ann said that at that moment Sue realized how much she had been ignoring me and it upset her...a lot. I was so amazed with this little baby in my arms. I was completely taken aback that Sue would let me hold and walk with the baby. I walked with her and I sang to her. I was in seventh heaven holding this precious little baby in my arms. I remembered my little bird and how much I missed Glenda. I wanted to be back in Glenda's arms so badly.

Shortly after this we went to the beach one night and watched the stars. It was all of us, even Teal. It was dark and we walked up and down the beach and played in the waves. When we got ready to leave, Teal was nowhere to be found. I was getting panicky; I loved Teal and I didn't want to leave without him. After all of us were loaded in the van, Sam said he would return and get Teal after he took us home. Sam said he didn't want us to whistle for Teal, but I did anyway and Teal came running. I was so happy and I thought Sam would be happy, too. He wouldn't have to make a trip back to find him; but instead of being happy, he yelled at me and spanked me. I was crying and I told Sam, "I don't like you! I want my daddy." I kept crying, "I want my daddy.......I want my daddy" all the way back home. Teal was my only friend. He listened to everything I said. Teal was the only one I trusted and I couldn't leave him behind. I loved Teal and he loved me. Obviously, Sam had no intention of bringing Teal back home. I figured that out after my spanking. After I figured that out, I was glad I had whistled for Teal. I don't know if I could have handled living there without my best friend. I don't think I could have handled another loss at that time in my life. I *needed* Teal.

After the beach incident, we had a family meeting. At first I thought it was pretty exciting because they gave me a robe and a belt to hold my pants up; but then they told us we were moving. I started crying and begged them to let us stay. I didn't like it there, but staying there was better than the unknown. The unknown was too scary to face. I felt bad for my sister because this was a perfect placement for her. Sue loved her and spent a lot of time with her and was teaching her a lot.

No one ever explained what foster care was, how long we would be away from our family or what the future held for us. It seemed that life for us was on a day-to-day basis. This led me to believe that I could never let my guard down because I never knew when we would be going to a "new" home. This left me with the impression that I could never allow myself to get too close to anyone because tomorrow I might not be a member of that family any longer. No explanation from DFCS meant my life would be in a "holding pattern" until I received notice that it was okay to become attached or truly involved. Until then, I had to live life as if tomorrow I would be moved to yet another home. This also meant that any feelings or emotions I thought I might have had, were now turned off. From this incident forward, there would be a very heavy chain around my heart and a huge padlock on it! I vowed to myself that I would never let anyone hurt me again.

Other than to inform us that we would be leaving, no one said anything more about it. Once again, no one spoke to us prior to our move, where we were going or what to expect. The next day a car came to pick us up and take us to our new home. Our few meager belongings were placed in black plastic bags and off we went into the unknown.

Chapter 9

My greatest fear was the unknown. How could I have done this? Why was I so unable to appreciate my surroundings that I could allow us to be taken to that place again....back into the black hole, that place of darkness, back into the world of the unknown?

I remember the long car ride and dreading another uncomfortable and painful adjustment period. We pulled up to a guard shack, and our driver talked with a guy in a uniform. The guard shack was at the front of a very large complex with extremely high fencing that had razor wire curled at the top. I remember this seeming rather odd and wondered if we were going to a different type of juvenile detention center. It was fenced in like our other juvenile placement except this one had a lot of buildings and people walking around and was much larger. I felt my heart jump into my throat as I wondered if we were going to be locked up again. Did I ruin it for everyone? I wanted to quickly go back to our other home and beg them to take us back. The unknown was just too hard to face and I didn't want to go there. I didn't have the energy to go there. I would do anything to keep from going there again, but I had no choice.

I was relieved when we turned onto one of the first streets as we entered this rather odd but large complex. I'm not sure I could have handled a long ride in this confined environment without completely loosing it. My heart was beating faster and faster with every millisecond that passed, and I was becoming shakier and shakier inside. I still remember the car taking a right shortly after we passed the guard shack. I watched children playing outside as we passed many double houses. I didn't remember ever seeing double houses like this and wondered if this was where the children were locked up at night. All of a sudden, we slowed down and came to a stop at one of the double houses. It looked just like all of the double houses on the road, but this row had that really high fencing behind it. I didn't understand where we were and could only think back to the juvenile detention center with that same fencing and how lonely of an existence that was. I was really scared as we walked up the sidewalk to the front door. I didn't want them to open the front door because I was afraid I would see a house full of sad children using vulgar and harsh language with handcuffs around their wrists and ankles. But instead, when they opened the door, this very nice lady with beautiful dark hair answered. She didn't speak with harsh, course words but had a soft angelic-like voice. I was so scared that I didn't hear what she said as I entered the front door. I just remember her voice having a calming effect and that was just what I needed at that moment. I think anything else would have caused me to burst into tears. I was terrified.

This placement was a different type of placement. Our new foster family lived on a military base. The Chases lived in a duplex with another family on the other side. This was the first time I had ever lived in a house with two families sharing the same building. It would have been nice if our driver had given us some information on our way. If he had explained about the Air Force Base and what an Air Force Base was, it would have eased a lot of the panic I was feeling, especially knowing we had lived in a juvenile detention center before.

On our first day when I walked in, I was surprised to see Sally, their oldest biological daughter, doing her math homework. What surprised me most was that she was doing her multiplications without using her fingers; she knew them all by heart. I complimented Sally and she could tell I was completely blown away. I was a little surprised and taken aback with Sally's comment to her mother. I remember Sally saying, "Well, if she's as smart as they say she is, how come she doesn't know her multiplication tables already?" I found her comment to be very hurtful. Not only by what was said, but how it was said and that it was said right after I had just walked into unfamiliar territory. No one had ever taught me to learn them by heart, not that I could have remembered them anyway. Or, maybe they did and I was so busy "surviving" that I wasn't aware of anything else but "survival." I made good grades and was proud of myself for that. As a foster child, you learn to pat yourself on the back for the lack of others doing it for you. I felt pretty beaten down, and this was only 2 minutes into day one. I just added this to the mound of hurt already stored inside a full and heavy heart.

I remember walking in, and it looked as if there were kids everywhere. It seemed as if there was a mound of little kids sitting or laying down, and they were all watching Gilligan's Island. The Chases had three biological children: Sally, Cathy and baby Ronnie. Then there were the five brothers: Larry, Barry, Bobby, Buddy and Billy. Then there was me, my sister and my brother soon followed. Later, we would be joined by Maggie and her brother. Pattie would come later and so would Scott. We had up to 14 children in a 4 bedroom duplex at one time. That would make for a family of 16 at our highest count.

Danny followed shortly, so it wasn't long before the three of us were together again. I don't remember anyone telling us in advance that Danny would be there. Either they didn't tell us or I was so consumed with another move that it didn't resonate with me. Either way, it no longer felt like family when we were together anyway. Gone was that family tie, or family bond, that siblings typically feel for each other. Gone was the sibling rapport and the typical sense of loyalty between family members. It was replaced instead with individual survival. Fear grappled me more than family ties, and I lived in extreme fear of my brother and my sister. Fear and survival now consumed me and defined my daily life.

There was a lot of crying from the little ones sometimes, but we all managed to mingle in one house. We weren't allowed to call our foster parents by their first names like in our first placement. So, instead of calling them Mr. and Mrs. Chase, we decided it would be easier to call them Mom and Dad instead. I didn't want to call them Mr. and Mrs. because it would be pretty obvious to everyone else that we were "different." I wasn't too happy about calling them Mom and Dad, either, because I didn't really even know them; but we settled on it anyway. I think this made it hard for me to connect with Mrs. Chase -- there was too much pain connected to the label "Mom." Every time I said it, all I could think of was all of the devastation, hurt and pain that came with calling someone "Mom." No one ever asked how I felt about this; no one ever asked about my feelings about anything. I was still unable to freely articulate how I felt nor did it feel safe to do so. So no one knew what was going on inside of me, inside of my young over-analytical head. I merely did as I was told. Every time I used the word "Mom," I longed for Glenda and the other mother I never knew. The word rang harsh in my ears, my head would fill with painful memories, and my heart would yearn for that amazing woman who once loved me . . . not the mother who birthed me, but the mother who became My Mommy.

We were allowed to watch television and play with toys there. That was a huge relief for me. We played on sports teams and rode our bikes to practices. I took sewing classes, went bowling and played on a softball team. We were on our bikes a lot and rode all over the base. I say "our" bikes, but they were their bikes that we were borrowing. As foster children, you never really own anything. As a foster child you are lucky to have clothes. But this was more of the type of life I was used to, just kind of on your own and doing your own thing. I liked this home environment much better. In this home, I could stay busy and keep my mind off of the bad memories. In this home, I could stay busy enough that the bad memories didn't have time to catch up with me. In this home, I could play with Sally's Barbies and pretend a beautiful life for her that we lived in together.

Except at night....at night the bad memories would keep me awake and they wouldn't leave me alone. I remember crying sometimes; they haunted me and caused my heart to grow dark and lonely. My heart felt as if it had a huge black hole, nothing could fill it and there was no one to talk to. I needed someone to help me understand this intense sadness I felt and teach me how to shake the incredible darkness that followed me every day. It was as if doom lingered over my head every day, all day long. If someone had talked to me about my feelings, they would have understood how incredibly lonely, lost and horrible I felt. They would have known how scared I was to wake up every day not knowing what the next day held for me. Then daylight would come once again and I would temporarily fill the darkness with activity, lots and lots of wonderful activity. I could survive another day as long as I kept busy enough to keep the darkness at bay.

While living with the Chases, I became an 8th grader which meant I rode a bus to a high school off base. I wasn't the oldest in the family, but I was in the highest grade and was the only one attending high school. I had always been the youngest in the family or one of the youngest. Suddenly, overnight I'm in the oldest child position. So now I was on my own for the very first time ever, and I found my new school very scary. The other kids were so much bigger than I was and seemed so much more mature. This was during the time of segregation and there was a lot of conflict between the races. I learned that a girl at my high school was stabbed in the bathroom; and the more I learned about my new school, the more it scared me. I had to go to the office one day during class to turn in some paperwork. I remember wearing a really cute little red, white and blue dress with high platform shoes. There was a senior guy standing alone in the hallway and I think he liked it, too. He whistled and called me over. Being the compliant person I was, I did as I was told, smiling all the while. I went over to him and he started saying pretty things about me and I continued smiling. I think I probably smiled a lot about these wonderful words I was hearing because he kept saying pretty things. I'd never had anyone tell me pretty things about myself and it felt really good. As he talked, he walked me over to a quiet and private-looking area. I was very naïve and unprepared for what was to come next. As he spoke his pretty little words, he started touching my face and playing with my hair. I started getting a little uncomfortable, but there wasn't any way out except to crawl under his legs. He started kissing me and giving me instructions on kissing back because I wasn't doing it right. Then he took my hand and put it someplace where he shouldn't have been putting it. I got really scared; but I didn't know what to do, so I just did as I was told to do as I had always done. As he started kissing my shoulder and putting his hand up my dress, the bell rang and high school students started flooding the hallways and private nooks. I was so thankful because I had no idea how to get out of a situation like that. No one had prepared me for anything like this, and I was no match for a guy who wanted to tell me pretty things about myself. I craved to hear the words, to have the affection; but I was completely unprepared for the cost. Actually, I was very naïve at what the cost really was. No one had told me about guys like this, about guys at all, or the facts of life. I was now in high school and had been told NOTHING about what was going on inside my body. I was totally and completely unprepared for this next phase of life. My maturity was still that of a little girl, an innocent, naïve little girl.

Life in my new home was moving along somewhat normally. Danny left shortly after he arrived. One day my sister, and Sally and I entered a beauty pageant. Our new foster mom knew how to sew, and she made me the most beautiful white dress I had ever seen. She even showed me how to make a matching white choker to go with it. I felt like a princess in my beautiful new white dress and platform heels. During the beauty contest, a Hispanic boy called out my name and said "Hello." He was from our old neighborhood, from when we lived with Dad, and was the boy who threw me out of the window when Dad shot at me. I waved at him and continued with the pageant. I was secretly hoping the little boy would tell my dad about his little girl in her beautiful white dress feeling like a princess in a beauty pageant. I was so happy and proud that day; I made it to the next level of the pageant. I was the girl everyone laughed at on the school bus and I made it to the next level of a beauty pageant. I felt beautiful for a change. The funny thing about this is that the girls who laughed at me on the school bus didn't make it to the next level, but I did. What was even funnier was that the next day, on the school bus, the girls were being teased because I passed them in the pageant. But it dawned on me later that day that the joke was still on me, but I couldn't understand why. I hadn't done anything or said anything to offend anyone. I couldn't figure out why the children on the bus kept making fun of me or the children in my classroom.

Then one day shortly after that, I heard my foster mom and some other woman talking and I heard my mom make a comment about not liking the smell of BO. She said it in a loud tone as if directing it to me, but I had no idea what she was talking about. I just knew whatever it was, it wasn't good. I could tell there was something about me she didn't care for, but I couldn't figure it out. I think she was probably trying to give me a hint without having to embarrass me and talk about it, but I had no idea what she was talking about. No one ever explained to me what BO was, and I'd never even heard of that word before that moment. I dared not ask because any time I questioned anything when I lived with my father, life would take a pretty nasty turn. So I never questioned anything, no matter what.

A couple of days later, there was a little girl at school who was being nice to me. I asked her why everyone kept laughing at me and making jokes about me. She explained everything to me; she told me what BO was and how to fix it. After I cleaned up and stopped smelling, I started having friends. By this time, my ego, self-esteem and self-confidence had taken quite a beating and I wasn't open to many friendships. I don't think I could have handled it, anyway. My only friend lived on the other side of our military duplex; his name was James.

I would ring James' doorbell and wake him up for school every morning. I remember his mother being happy with our friendship and thanked me for taking such good care of James. We were just friends and I never thought of him as anything but a good friend. It felt nice to have someone I could talk to, just a little bit. James often invited me to tag along with him and his cousin when they went off. It was nice having someone to just hang around with and not have to answer too many questions. James never asked any questions about my past; he just let me enjoy our friendship and merely gave me a gentle place to just quietly be. That was exactly what I needed, just a quiet place to be with no pressures, no bad memories, just an occasional quiet conversation if I wanted it. If not, he would just quietly sit there and hold my hand.

It wasn't long after the pageant that we got news about our foster family being transferred overseas. This left us in a bit of a dilemma, for the first time EVER we were asked about our feelings concerning our situation. DFCS explained what this meant for us and asked if we wanted to go to Europe with the Chases. My sister and I said yes, and they moved forward with severing parental rights. I didn't know what severing parental rights meant, but everyone seemed excited about it so it sounded like a good thing. My father not in my life was a very good thing!

I don't remember my dad attending the court hearing when they severed his rights. I don't think he really cared; we never heard from him or saw him, anyway. A couple of times we visited with my grandmother, but Dad was never there. At Christmastime when we visited my grandmother, my aunts in Columbia bought Christmas gifts and brought them over to Grandmother's. Otherwise, we would have gone without. I remember that Christmas so well because they bought me the prettiest ruby ring. I wore it every day with pride until it flung off my hand when I threw the softball at a game. I tried to find it, but it was lost forever. I remember one July we were visiting my grandmother while the Chases were on vacation, and my Aunt Joann made me a strawberry cake with strawberry icing for my birthday. I think this was my very first birthday cake ever. It was really good and I was so blown away that she would do something like this for my birthday. They were so good to us and Dad was so lucky to have them. His sisters weren't anything like him. They were as caring and as loving as they could be in a situation like this.

Dad had remarried and started a new family. He forgot about his other children and started a new family with a new wife. He threw us away and started a whole new life. I really didn't care; I liked my life and I enjoyed living where I was. I didn't feel an emotional connection to anyone, but I liked my environment. I knew I was safe and that was good enough for me. But how can someone just discard family #1 as if they never existed and simply start family #2? How could someone be that incredibly cold and heartless?

In the Spring of 1976, we became the first foster children ever allowed out of the United States with foster parents. It was one of the happiest days of my life. This meant I never had to see my real family ever again if I didn't want to, and I didn't for many years. I no longer had to visit with my real family and I felt so relieved. Only now, could the healing begin. Only now, could I finally put the bad memories behind me and focus on the future. I couldn't do that when I had to go back and forth. You can't focus on the future when you are constantly pulled back and forth like that. You can't build a relationship with your foster parents when you constantly have to go back and forth. Every time you go back to your foster family you feel like you are betraying your real family and you feel dirty. Every time you visit your real family you feel like you are letting your foster parents down. You are in a no-win situation and you feel the pressures of it every day. The weight I was carrying around was so heavy, the burdens were more than I could bear, and the thought of eliminating some of them felt like angels singing in my ears.

In my case, I didn't want to visit my real family. Visiting them brought up too many painful memories, and the only person I could take it out on was my foster mother. For my sister, it was me who got her anger. My sister probably would have literally killed me if I had taken all of that anger out on her. I needed someone to talk to -- a therapist, a mentor. There was no one to direct all of that anger at except for my foster mother. I wasn't a bad child, I didn't really do bad things; but I was very condescending and would not allow my foster mom to build a relationship with me. I think I was too afraid to build a relationship with her. I still missed Glenda too much and the thought of being ripped out of her arms, was just too much for me to risk again. I also think I was afraid that if I got close to Momma Chase, I would never be able to recover from another tragic loss and it would send me over the edge. Even as a child, I had realized I was teetering on the edge of something horrible when I lost Glenda; she was such a devastating loss to me. I think she was the last person I truly allowed into my heart for many, many years. Something terrible happened to my heart when they ripped me out of Glenda's arms. I think my heart died that day, because I couldn't feel it anymore after that.

It took a little time for us to prepare for our new adventure. We still had to get our passports and our shots. The typhoid shot was the worst . . . it left my arm really sore. I still had to get my school transcripts, but I was so thankful to be leaving my new high school. We watched as kids left our home, family by family until we dwindled down to the family we were going to be in Holland. The Chases and their three children were going, my sister, me and another foster child named Pattie. We were a family of eight going to Holland to live. Although the true impact of what was about to happen never really set in, I think I was happy about the decision. It was really hard to decide how I felt about it, because I had become pretty numb inside by that time. It felt as if I was merely doing life on "auto pilot." I would muddle through day-to-day life, but I don't remember feeling emotions or feelings during this time. To me, moving thousands of miles away felt like I was just going to yet another home across town. I was excited about a new adventure, but I don't think I really felt any certain way about the move. It just was what it was -- words that we were moving to another country. The only thing on my mind was that I wasn't going to have to face the unknown. My only goal in life was to maintain continuity; thus, never having to face the unknown again. Staying in this family environment and not having to move to another was the only thing I could focus on and nothing beyond. Everyday revolved around doing whatever it took to keep from facing the "unknown" ever again. I remember Mom Chase showing us an article in the newspaper about the court's decision to allow us to leave the United States and it being a first of its kind. I smiled about it, but it still hadn't set in. This was to be my very first airplane ride, but yet I lacked the excitement ordinary children have about a major new experience like this. DFCS asked us if we wanted to go and, of course, I said yes. I didn't want to move to yet another family and go back into the world of the unknown. No one asked the hard probing questions or explained what moving to Holland really meant, which was totally okay with me. But now I am curious: this was such a huge decision, yet no one really sat down and talked to us in depth about a decision of this magnitude. I have no regrets about going, but DFCS should have explained how they would stay in contact, how we could contact them if we had an issue, and what to expect upon our return. No one ever talked to me about any of these things. It seems as if children have absolutely no rights once they enter the world of foster care. You merely become a lifeless pawn moved from space to space with little care or regard for your will or wants, likes or dislikes. It's about merely trying to find a free space to move the lifeless pawn yet again, and again.

Chapter 10

April came around and it was finally time for our new journey. Last April I was a broken battered little girl holding a dead bird and spewing hateful words at God. This April I find myself flying on the wings of a man-made craft to a new life and a new start. It was out with the old, and in with the new!

It all began with a nice warm, sunny South Carolina day as we gathered the rest of our belongings and headed to the airplane. We were all happy faces and smiles as we boarded the biggest airplane I had ever seen. As I sat down in my seat, I looked at the inside of the airplane, taking in the newness of it all. This was my very first flight; and now that I think back on it, I was strangely calm. There was no fright, no nervousness, only calmness. Although this was my first airplane flight and my first trip out of the United States, it felt just like any other day. When the airplane took off, there were no jitters, just calmness. It was as if I subconsciously knew that distance would serve me well. The further I flew from all of that horror and pain, the better I felt. Maintaining continuity and moving thousands of miles away from my father was as close as I could get to heaven.

The first break on our long journey was a quick stop in Canada. We stopped only to refuel the plane and restock supplies. Although we were safely and comfortably tucked inside the airplane, you could feel the bitter cold as it seeped into the cabin. I remember thinking, "Wow, this is cold!" but it wasn't long before we were on our way and were once again toasty warm.

Again, all I felt was internal numbness. It was a long flight to Germany; but we were able to sleep, so I slept most of this last part of the trip. I remember that what seemed odd was that I was no longer plagued with the bad memories that haunted me when I slept. It seemed as if they stayed behind in the United States, that somehow when I boarded that airplane the bad memories refused to follow me. I don't remember having the bad memories plague my sleep anymore after we left the United States. It was as if I was finally set free.

When we landed in Frankfurt and got off the plane, once again I was shocked at how cold it was. We had been told to bring coats which we thought was silly, but now I was thankful I had one! I was shocked to see so much snow and ice still on the ground. We had often visited Tennessee when it was cold, but I had never been in the cold for a long period of time and not as cold as this cold was. It was April and I didn't realize other countries got this cold in April. It was springtime in South Carolina where we just left 70 degree weather, but here it was below freezing. I realized then that this was going to take some getting used to.

It was about a 2½ hour drive from the airport in Frankfurt, Germany, to where we lived in Holland. There were so many people in our family that the military had to send a small bus to pick us up at the airport and take us to our temporary home. I remember it being a long, cold ride. When we arrived at our destination, we were surprised to be living in a type of European hotel. Our European hotel was more like an American bed and breakfast inn. We and the other families on the same floor had separate bedrooms, but we all shared the same bathroom and shower room. The toilet room and the shower were located in different rooms, which again was unfamiliar to me. We lived there for about 30 to 60 days. I don't remember exactly how long, just that it was a long time. At first, it was great to live in a hotel. We ate out every day, there were no dishes to wash, and someone else cleaned our rooms for us. I remember thinking, "Wow, now this is the way to live!"

Our first morning there, we were pleasantly surprised when we went downstairs for breakfast and sitting on the table in front of us were dishes of chocolate sprinkles --you know, the ones that we decorate cakes and cookies with here in America. In Europe they have small bowls of chocolate sprinkles on the table where you can put as much as you want on top of your toast. Well, you know what I had for breakfast every morning. Toast with lots and lots of milk chocolate sprinkles!!!!!! I thought I had died and gone to heaven.

The weather though, that was going to take some time to get used to. Even though we had been there for a month or so, it was still very cold outside. At home it would have been going into summer weather, but there it was still barely Spring weather. I had no idea the weather in other countries could be so different. Although the weather was drastically different, I still loved my environment and the new sense of emotional freedom I was feeling. I loved the different look that Holland had -- the houses, the streets, the people. It felt very quaint and rather homey. Something inside me was changing, ever so slowly, yet changing. I think I was feeling a little bit of happiness. It felt as if a huge weight had been lifted off my shoulders and I was finally allowing myself to feel enjoyment, which was an unfamiliar feeling for me. I was finally starting to ever so slowly feel a little bit of emotion inside my heart. I was so shocked that I was actually starting to feel enjoyment from my new surroundings. I finally felt free to feel and free enough to start enjoying life. I even started talking more, and I don't remember the stuttering being much of an issue anymore. I think I felt less nervous and I wasn't anxious and all shaky inside like before. I think this might have had something to do with my stuttering problem.

We eventually moved out of our hotel and into a beautiful European home. Our house had three floors and was a traditional European home. The weather was still very cold; but, in time, we got used to the cold environment, both inside and out. Mom Chase let me have a room to myself on the third floor. The only drawback about this room was that there was no heat in it. I gladly sacrificed the heat to have a room to myself. I had never had my very own room before, except in the juvenile detention center. A couple of months after I was in my room, I accidently found a secret wall that opened up where people must have stayed during the war. As I entered this cold eerie room, I found a very old baby doll lying on the floor. Her clothes were tattered and she had a band aid on her right foot. As I stood hunched over in this cold dark space, I remember feeling sadness for the people who must have lived in there. I had read <u>The Diary of Ann Frank</u>, and it was so incredible to have the opportunity to marry the book to the feeling of standing inside this hidden room where people once hid for their lives just like the book described. I think this moment was a pivotal moment for me. I stood there with my eyes closed trying to feel their emotions, the sadness of the people who lived in that secret room. I remember feeling sorry for them. They lived in a room where you had to hunch over to stand, where it was dark and very, very cold. I think feeling their sadness helped me to allow a little bit of feeling back into my life. I think it reminded me how thankful I was to have the life that I had. Standing inside that room, I knew someone else knew the sadness that lived in my heart, someone else knew how hopeless and helpless I felt. It felt good to know that someone else could truly understand how empty I felt inside. But at the same time, this also helped me to realize how lucky and blessed I was. I was a foster child who had read a book in America and here I am a few months later standing in a secret room in Holland relishing an experience that few children will ever have and an experience that no other foster child will probably ever have again. The magnitude of that blessing surrounded me with an amazing feeling that I was somehow special to God. I left that room feeling a little better about myself that day.

Normal life came much easier for me in Holland. I was much happier living in Holland than I had been in the United States. I think having that much distance between me and my family took a huge burden off my shoulders. I also think it may have helped tremendously to know DFCS would no longer be pulling up any moment to take me to another unknown environment. Although I still didn't belong to the Chase's, I was far away enough that DFCS couldn't come just anytime they wanted to. Or maybe it was because I was so afraid of my father that I feared living life that close to him. Was I so burdened with "the occasional visit" that I couldn't be happy living there? We lived over 100 miles from where my father lived but only a few miles from where most of the major trauma occurred. Did living so close to those events cause me to be unable to move on? I'm not sure what was holding me back from letting go, but living in Holland brought out a whole new Helen. I talked much more, I made friends and I almost felt somewhat like an ordinary child, not a foster child. Maybe it was that there we didn't live in a "foster world" as in the United States since we were the only foster children around. It was much easier to blend in as an ordinary child instead of standing out as a foster child. Maybe wearing an obvious label caused me that much trauma and stress. Whatever the reason, here I could pretend I was the Chase's child and no one knew any different. It felt nice to be all bubbly and happy, although it did get me into trouble a little more. But that was okay, it was typical teenager stuff and the Chase's were being typical parents of typical teenagers. Life was good…life was really good.

One day I sat on my bed in my very own room staring at the only personal possessions I owned that made it from my dad's home --my Small Fry Queen trophy and a picture that was taken of me after being crowned. As I sat staring at my picture, I was trying to grasp the fact that this little girl and I were one and the same. I was thinking about the horror that this little girl had lived; and now with my new life, it seemed impossible that I was that little girl in the picture. But here, in front of me, was proof that that little girl was indeed me. Then all of a sudden I saw a picture in my head; I think I may have been daydreaming. Although I never allowed thoughts about the future or what I wanted to be or do with my life, for some reason I saw myself as a grown woman dressed in nice slacks, a nice shirt and heels walking in the front foyer of a beautiful home. I think I may have been answering the door. In my dream I could tell it was my house and I felt very confident and sure of myself as I walked down the foyer of this beautiful home. It put a smile on my face and the dream or vision was gone as quickly as it came. I never allowed myself to think about my future. It was all I could do to live one day at a time because the future was too hard and too painful to think about. Anytime I thought of the future, there were so many unanswered questions that I couldn't handle it; and I would make myself put it out of my head and just concentrate on the moment. I think I must have been in survival mode. All I could think about was making it to the next day. Although I was no longer plagued with bad memories, I still felt the need to feel ready for impending disaster every day. But it was nice to know that I must have felt safe enough for my mind to leap into the future, if only for a moment in time. This was progress. However, I was very surprised to see myself as a "confident" woman, as there was not a hint of confidence whatsoever within my body or mind, and I wondered if I would ever be able to overcome this. The shyness was so painful, and I attributed all of my issues to that. I never realized I lacked self-confidence or self-esteem until I was much older. At this stage in life, I had no idea what those were nor had I ever heard anyone speak of them, much less realized it was something major that I was lacking and desperately needed to work on.

My 9th grade year was probably the best and most fun year of my life. I was feeling more like a normal kid with a normal kid life. We were in a different country and nobody knew I was nobody's child. But for some reason, I still had trouble connecting with Mom Chase. Speaking from my perspective as a teenager, I think we got along pretty well; but my actions were very cold, emotionless. I think I was a pretty compliant child. I do know I did have the occasional teenager issues but lacked any real relationship emotion, if that makes sense. I think Mom Chase may have felt I was angry at her and, in a way, I probably was. Although I felt more normal, you can't just forget everything that happened in a life like mine overnight. I think Mom thought the anger was directed towards her, but I think it was mainly a coping technique to keep me from getting too close. Or maybe it was the fact I didn't have anyone to help me understand my feelings, and she was the only one I could take them out on. I don't think I was a bad child, I don't think I was a defiant child, but maybe a bit of a cocky and cold child. However, I don't think Mom realized how big of a positive step I had made. I don't think Mom realized that talking, having friends and having fun was a HUGE step for me. I don't think Mom understood the huge positive impact she did have on me. I do know I didn't tell her or show her. I didn't know how to or that I was supposed to. I'm sure I came across as if I only took and never gave back, but no one had ever taught me how to be a daughter or how to accept love or how to give back.

I will never forget my very first class trip. The entire 9th grade class went to Amsterdam on a field trip. We took a train from Brunssum to Amsterdam. On the European rails they serve beer to anyone, even minors, as there was no drinking age limit over there. Needless to say, we were all drinking beer on the way back home. A few days later my sister heard the talk at school and told my mom what happened. When Mom Chase found out about the trip, she asked me about it. I told her that I drank beer but that I wasn't drunk. Mom went across the street and bought some beer from the fritz stand. She made me drink them and write my name after each beer I finished. I don't really remember exactly how many I drank, but I wrote my name with no problem after each one. I'm sure it seemed like more than it truly was. Drinking beer in front of your mom with spectators, I'm sure every minute seemed like hours! Mom had me sit there for a while longer after I finished the final beer and then she let me go and take a bath. What she never knew for many years was that after I got upstairs, while I ran my bath water, I got very sick. Needless to say, I can't stand beer to this day! I think Mom may have called the school because I heard kids saying that my parents were going to sue the school. I never found out what that was all about, I just wanted it to go away. I do know that this was the end of my "normal" childhood. The cat was out of the bag. Once again everyone knew that I was different and that I was nobody's child, and life at school would never be the same.

Mom Chase was a wonderful seamstress and she taught me how to sew. I loved sewing and making pretty clothes. In time I became a pretty good seamstress, nowhere near as good as Mom, but I could sew fairly well. I actually won a contest at school with a shirt I made for my sister; this was a countrywide contest, so there were many competitors. My sister must have really liked her shirt a lot because she wore it all the time. It made me feel all warm and fuzzy inside because she liked it so much. I enjoyed making my sister happy, but I felt a great sadness because she didn't seem to like me very much.

While I was still in the 9th grade, I made Sally's and my sister's formal Homecoming dresses. Mom had made a beautiful long blue dress for me with pretty white daisy lace the year previous, so I was going to wear the one I already had. I had finished making Sally's, but while I was in the middle of making Vicky's dress, she got into trouble and was restricted from Homecoming. I think she was on restriction for kissing in public, though I'm not sure. Sally seemed happy with the way her dress turned out, and I was happy that she seemed pleased.

Mom and Dad were very strict with us; and my number one offense, I think, was the kissing in public and maybe grades that were not up to standards. What I really liked about the rules there was that Mom and Dad Chase told us what the rules were and what the punishment would be if we broke the rules. They were strict rules and the consequences were pretty harsh, but Mom and Dad let us know the expectations up front and were extremely consistent with the consequences. That was something I could work with -- I didn't have to wonder. I knew in advance and in time I knew I had no choice but to conform or else I would suffer the consequences. I also knew that they would find out anything I did that I wasn't supposed to do, so after a time, I was extremely compliant. Dad never yelled -- he talked to us and then restricted us. I really think the extreme consistency is what turned me around. I knew Dad would never give in; and if I didn't want to be restricted, I had no choice but to conform. I got caught kissing in public a couple of times and that carried a 6 week restriction per incident. I once brought home a C- in Algebra and was restricted for 9 weeks until I brought the grade up. My boyfriend at the time was very smart and he tutored me. My C- became an A the next nine weeks and remained there for the rest of the year. However, the boyfriend didn't because he decided to put his hand up my shirt as Mom came around the corner and she saw what he had done. He could be a little pushy about that, and I didn't quite know how to deal with it.

Boy, did I get into trouble for that one! For starters I lost my boyfriend. I didn't understand it then, but I probably would have done the same for my daughter if I ever caught the same thing happening. I wasn't promiscuous, but I had a hard time telling him "No." I had spent years complying to keep people happy. To suddenly turn that off was very hard, but it was something that had to be done or the end result could have been disastrous. Mom took me over to his parents' house and had a talk with them. I think it made Mom even madder when they didn't take it very seriously and insinuated that he was merely a boy experimenting like all boys do. Mom was talking about filing statutory rape charges, but I think she was just really angry. After a time, it all faded away. Needless to say, that never happened again. It was all very embarrassing and was all over the school. I don't think I had very many high school boyfriends after that. After my humiliation was spread all over school, I started dating GI's instead. The boys at school wouldn't date me anymore. My past had become a big topic of conversation and my sister was more than happy to share the details with almost anyone who listened. I often overheard guys saying, "She's been through enough, I don't want to cause her anymore hurt"; or, "We would just be dating; and at some point she's going to be hurt, and I don't want to be the cause of that."

One of the biggest differences between my sister and I was that she couldn't hold a secret and told everyone everything they ever wanted to know . . . and a whole lot more. She knew no boundaries. I, on the other hand, could keep a secret until doomsday and didn't want anyone to know anything about my past. I was adamant about never using my sorrowful past as a tool to win over hearts with sympathy. I wanted to earn people's hearts and respect with *who* I was.

During our stay in Holland, we started going to church. We attended a small church that was started by five families, Emmanuel Baptist Church in Kerkrade, Holland. This was all new for me. I enjoyed going to church and enjoyed meeting the families we would spend most of our free time with. Living in Holland was perfect for someone like me. There was no American television, so we spent most of our free time playing sports, playing cards with the family, going to church and being a part of a church "family," or reading. For me, this was perfect. When you couple that with parents who never argued in front of the kids, rules and expectations noted from the very beginning and delivered with firm consistency, this perfect situation laid a strong foundation that would define who I am today. Although there were still a lot of major missing pieces in my life and social skill deficits, this foundation was a major win for a child like me.

We were allowed to go on our very first church retreat with the other kids. Since my sister and Sally were not yet in the 9th grade, they went on the retreat first. It was a ski retreat. Mom and Dad bought us all ski outfits to wear on our trip. I went the following week with the high school kids. I had so much fun. For the first time ever I was able to just hang out with kids my age and enjoy being a teenager. I think I smiled A LOT that weekend. I loved spending time with my church family. They were more like my family than just a "church" family. This was the first time I was allowed to go away with girlfriends from church and just have as much fun as possible.

We were in church every Sunday morning, every Sunday evening and every Wednesday evening. Church became the center of our family. We often went on retreats and had a blast every time we did. We stayed in old castles and bomb shelters on our retreats. Mom started a puppet ministry, and we had fun with the puppets and often sang in church. Gone were the horrific memories of yesterday, and I was able to concentrate 100% on my life for a change. The only thing that held me back was my sister and her anger towards me. I was afraid of her, and I knew never to push her emotionally and never ever touch her physically. I knew if I ever got her to "that" point that she might not be able to hold back, and I was afraid of what she might truly be capable of. She was the only thread left of my old life. For some reason, my sister didn't have the same attachment to me that I had to her. When we became foster children and I didn't have family anymore, at least I had her; and although she didn't feel the same about me, I was okay with that. I truly felt that someday she would come to love me. I thought someday she would stop degrading me, belittling me and taking all of her anger out on me and come to love the little sister that I was. I think I might understand it now, but I couldn't figure it out then. Only after I had a foster child of my own did I come to understand Reactive Attachment Disorder. I truly feel both she and I suffered from an attachment disorder. And to be honest, I truly feel all foster children suffer from some degree of Post Traumatic Stress Disorder as well as an Attachment Disorder. You don't rip children out of their "abnormal" lives and toss them into the unknown without causing some degree of trauma. It is finally documented that foster children are more than twice as likely to suffer from PTSD than veterans returning from war.

One day we three older girls were making pizza for dinner and I had on a pair of my sister's pants. She told me to take them off; but because my hands were all sticky from pizza dough, I told her I would in just a minute. She said, "No...take them off now." I, of course, responded with a "No"; so she decided to pull them off of me right then and there. She pulled them off of me in front of company. Both her and Sally's boyfriends were at our house for dinner. So there I stood in my panties in front of two teenage boys. I got really mad, and somehow she ended up in the bathroom where I pushed her. When she fell on the toilet, she hurt her thumb. I was terrified when I saw that look in her eyes. I could tell I had hurt her. She said a few potty words and that I had broken her thumb. I didn't actually break her thumb, but I saw a look in her eyes that freighted me. I knew she was out to seriously harm me and that I had better watch my step. My mom and dad saw that look, too; and I think they felt the same feeling I felt because when they left the house, they made her go with them.

I don't think it was too long after that incident when I woke up one day and my sister was no longer there. Although I felt relieved, I also felt a deep, dark emptiness deep within my soul. It was so sad that she could never feel for me the same strong attachment that I felt for her. I loved her so much and looked up to her. I remember thinking she was such a strong person and that she always found a way to get what she wanted. She had a great relationship with Mom and Sally and I longed to be just like her. I wanted to be vocal, outgoing, and strong just like her. What made me the saddest was that I never got to say goodbye. She and I had always done life together, but she was gone in a blink of an eye in the middle of the night. Someone stole my sister like a thief in the night; I woke up and she was gone. My sister was gone; she existed no more....I closed my eyes and I thought for a minute. Was she ever really there, or was my mind merely playing tricks on me? People don't take siblings away in the middle of the night without saying anything.... or do they? How could it be that no one cared enough for me to prepare me for that moment? I know I was thousands of miles away, but someone talked to Mom to make arrangements for Vicky, so why didn't someone talk to me at the same time? I was still a ward of the State of South Carolina and they had an obligation to me. They didn't speak one word to me after I left the United States. Someone from DFCS should have made monthly phone calls to me, but they never did. After my sister left, I fell into a very deep depression. The one person I had done life with was now gone in the blink of an eye. This shook the foundation and core of my inner being until there was nothing left but shambles. How was I supposed to trust anyone after this?

Several months after my sister left, I started the 10th grade and my psychology teacher said, "Helen, last year I called you an incurable nuisance; but this year you're too quiet. *Actually, you're scary quiet."* This Helen who suddenly became a beautiful butterfly the day she stepped off the bus in Holland died as quickly as she arrived. A quiet anger and loneliness would consume my body and I felt as if I were dead inside. I knew it was the best thing for me, but losing the last piece of family I had ever known would prove to be more than I could handle. This would be that "last straw," and I once again felt emotionally numb inside. Again, there was no one to talk to. Although I was never able to share with my sister as sisters do, she was that little piece of consistency which I had used to help center me. With no one to quietly share my grief with, all I could do was let it out little by little on my mom. I was so angry with her, quietly angry. Why didn't she tell me, why didn't she allow me to say goodbye? Why didn't she prepare me for one of the most devastating moments in my life? Why didn't she tell me and cry with me then hug me and tell me it was going to be okay? I now felt I would never be able to trust this family with my heart. It instantly turned to stone and there was nothing I could do about it. I became quietly bitter and extremely angry.

Dad worked a lot and Mom was the one who got most of my frustration. Mom handled almost everything in our home and was the bad cop. Since Dad wasn't around as much as Mom, he was able to maintain the status of good cop and I adored him. Unfortunately, I made this quietly very clear to Mom. Poor Mom got the brunt of all my anger.

Although I didn't do bad stuff, I was a little mouthy when I was given commands or would give a look that could kill. My grades fell . . . not failing, mind you, but I didn't do as well as I was capable of. I only did what I had to do to get by and no more. I didn't care anymore. For years to come, I would merely muddle through each day. My heart had become stone; it felt absolutely nothing anymore. Church would become my one saving grace. My church family would become the only place where I felt safe, loved, and valued.

I now spent a lot of my spare time reading alone in my room, and we spent a lot of time at church. I found comfort spending time with the other families in our church. One family stood out to me above all the rest -- The Campbell family. I will never forget the day Mrs. Campbell reached out and gave me a hug. I think she must have seen that I really needed a hug. I remember the smile on her face and the sparkle in her eyes as she reached out and cradled me in her arms. It wasn't too long after I lost my sister, and I was so desperate for someone to help me feel wanted and valued. I needed to feel loved. When she gave me that incredible hug, all I could think was I couldn't remember the last time someone had hugged me like that. Kathie had cradled me in her arms and Glenda had held me in her lap and hugged me goodnight; but I couldn't ever remember someone just holding me and cradling me in their arms like that. It felt so good and I didn't want it to end. I wanted to stay there forever. At that moment, I just wanted to crawl into her lap and stay in those warm loving arms forever. Mrs. Campbell was so sweet and so kind. I loved her so much, but I don't think she ever really knew how I felt about her.

Don't get me wrong, I was blessed with a good family; but I felt that Mom and I didn't get along very well. It seems to me that many of the things I did or said weren't right, and maybe my internal anger showed in my actions and words. I don't know. I can only see these things from my perspective, a teenager in a constant state of trauma. All I know is that I didn't often hear nice things about myself -- not that I heard a lot of bad things -- but I needed to hear that what I did was right so that I could keep doing that instead of the "bad" things I was often doing. I thought I looked a little like Mom and I liked that. We looked as if we could be family, and that often put a smile on my face. I thought Mom Chase was a very pretty woman and I loved the way she smelled, but I didn't know how to tell her any of that. All she got from me was the bad stuff. How could I love her when I couldn't love myself? How could I value her if I knew no value of my own? I wanted her to hurt as much as I hurt inside. I needed for someone to understand how miserable and dark I felt inside. I felt so lonely and helpless, and I didn't know how to make it go away. Maybe I thought if I could make her feel as bad as I did, that she could finally understand how I felt . . . every day.

Mom and Dad let me go over to a girlfriend's house after church one day and spend the night with her. Lynne had a beautiful house; and when I went into her room, I was surprised at how beautiful it was. It was very feminine and all of her furniture matched. I decided then and there that one day I was going to have bedroom furniture like that. Lynne's mom was so sweet and I watched as they shared mother and daughter time. It brought tears to my eyes to see how they interacted with each other, how they talked and enjoyed each other's company. I watched them intently from afar. I wanted to be Lynne so badly; she was athletically talented and everyone loved her. She was always laughing and having fun. To this day, I can close my eyes and see an older, young Lynne laughing and beaming all over. I loved to hear her laugh and I still do; it makes me feel all warm inside. Even today, every time I hear her laugh, it quickly takes me back to the years of yesterday and it always brings tears to my eyes, the memories of yesterday.

One day to my surprise, Mom told me I had a telephone call, so I went down to the phone. A little girl from school had called to talk to me. This was the first time I had ever been on the phone with anyone that I could remember. I remember feeling scared because I didn't know what I was supposed to say to this little girl. No one had ever taught me anything about communication or how to have a conversation with friends. As the little girl chatted on, I thought I had better say something, so I repeated what she was saying. She said that her mother talked a lot on the phone and I said back to her, "Yeah, my mom talks a lot on the phone, too." I didn't think there was much harm in what I said. It wasn't true, but I managed to say something back to the little girl and was rather proud of myself. When I got off the phone, Mom Chase came upstairs to my room and was very angry with me. I didn't really understand the harm behind what I had said. No one had taught me about other people's feelings, how to empathize with others, or how to have a conversation with other people. Mom didn't stop to think about my lack of social skills and use it as a teaching moment. Instead, she shut the door on any chance she had of becoming someone I could trust. The lack of intense education and training from DFCS *before* ever becoming a foster family was setting us up for failure, yet again.

What I needed was to feel loved, wanted and valued. I needed to hear a little bit of positive reinforcement. Although Mom may have been trying to give me what I needed emotionally, I may not have been willing to see it at the time. My reality was that I may not have been seeing things the way she may have been. I was angry with Mom, and it felt like Mom was angry with me most of the time for being angry with her. To me, it felt like a never-ending cycle. Although that might not have been reality, it was my reality and it was real to me. I needed someone to talk to who could help me understand everything I was feeling . . . and there was *no one.*

Dad loved to play cards and we would get together, us older girls, with some of our friends and we would all play cards together. Sometimes it would just be Dad, Sally and me. It was something we did often and something we all enjoyed doing together. Mom kept the little ones occupied, so this often left her out of our family time. I think this type of situation allowed me to bond with Dad, but not with Mom. As an adult, I can see where Mom really didn't get many positive building blocks to try to build a relationship with me; I had much more in common with Dad in those days. It must have been terribly hard for her to see how I treated Dad and then how I treated her.

Around my 16th birthday, we took a family trip to Italy. On my birthday, I remember climbing the stairs in the leaning tower of Pisa and thought to myself, "Wow, what an opportunity for someone like me!" I was mesmerized by the architecture and beautiful paintings in the chapel. Throughout the hallways were displays of paintings by Peter Paul Rubens, and they were absolutely gorgeous. Then we visited the Coliseum and I stood where people had stood thousands of years before me. I remember knowing how special that moment was: I was a foster child from America, and here I stood thousands of miles away on my 16th birthday touching marble that had been touched by people thousands of years before me, people who lived during the time of Christ. How was it possible that someone like me could possibly be experiencing something like this?!

Outside of the chapel, a lady was selling beautiful white handcrafted shawls. Mom said I could have any one I wanted since it was my birthday. I remember feeling very special that day and I didn't want the day to end. I remember wearing my beautiful white shawl around my shoulders throughout Italy the rest of the day along with a big, huge smile on my face.

Time went on and I participated in sports, although my game was not what my game had been. I felt as if I was doing life on empty after my sister left. I felt as if I was always sad; I think I was probably in a constant state of depression. I participated in church events and, to be honest, I think church was the one outlet where I felt at my best. I felt at home when I was at church. There was always a comfort about church and our church family. I didn't often allow myself to be happy or to show happiness outside of our church environment anymore. I remember this making Mom pretty upset. She would say something about my sadness, and I think she thought it was a put-on for other people to feel sorry for me. What she didn't realize was that I *was* that sad inside. There was a deep, dark hole that consumed my entire being; and I had no one to help me understand or teach me how to deal with it.

I realized I had enough high school credits to graduate early, and I decided to get out of school as quickly as I could. Walking through the hallways of our school reminded me of all the bad stuff, and I think the staff felt sorry for me because of my situation. I just wanted to be done with it and out of the environment that reminded me of the bad stuff every day. I think I thought that, if I graduated, I would have to go back to the United States so I could go to college or get a job. I thought that after I graduated I would have to go back to DFCS, back to where my sister was. I wanted to run from the darkness, but I was also terrified of the unknown. I didn't know which way to run, what to do or how to feel. I desperately needed someone to guide me, someone to believe in me. Foster parents can't do that; it takes someone outside of the authority circle. I needed a mentor --not a year or two mentor, but a lifelong mentor, a "Life Partner." I needed one relationship that would be constant because everything else in my life was a continuously changing variable. I desperately needed one constant who could advocate for me and who could be that one person who made sure I didn't fall through the cracks, someone who could make sure I was receiving all of the services I needed to transition into adult life successfully. If I had had a life partner looking out for my wellbeing, she would have known from our interactions that I desperately needed a therapist in my life. So much was going on inside my head, yet I was completely unable to articulate the feelings. It never crossed my mind that this wasn't normal. It never ever even crossed my mind that the inability to voice my feelings wasn't normal. I know this must seem odd or impossible, but it truly NEVER crossed my mind. Did I not have the words to articulate, or did the fear of using words freeze me to the point of lacking the ability to do so? Maybe it was a combination of both. I don't understand how I could have allowed this to control my entire life. But it did, and I suffered horribly for it. This inability truly caused me to live a confined life way into my adult years.

On June 14,1979, I graduated from high school two years early. I was 16 when I graduated, and I was the only person in my immediate family to earn a high school diploma.

After graduation I talked about returning to the United States, but Mom said I would be too much of a handful for MawMaw (my foster mother's mom). I had mailed a college application to Bauder College for a degree in fashion designing and was accepted. I thought I remember showing this to Mom, but maybe I was too scared of the unknown to show it to her. I didn't quite understand what MawMaw had to do with me going to college because I figured the Chase's wouldn't have to worry about me anymore, but I never questioned it. Besides, I'm not sure I was ready to be that independent; I was still in a VERY fragile state of mind. I think Mom knew that as well and was doing what she felt was best for me. Although part of me wanted to go back to The States, a part of me was too afraid to face the unknown again.

Shortly after graduation, on July 5, 1979, I turned 17 years old. I don't remember where I had been; but when I came home, Mom had scattered several Seventeen magazines on the top of my bed. I thought that was a really sweet birthday surprise. I felt a twinge of closeness with Mom that day. I can still see that smile on her face when she realized she had made me happy. Maybe I was so miserable inside that I was determined that Mom wasn't going to bring happiness to me, or maybe I didn't feel I was worthy of happiness. I so desperately needed someone to help me understand "me."

Several weeks after I graduated, Dad Chase came home with a moped. I had never even thought about having one, so it was a real surprise when he said it was for me. Now I had a way to get around town by myself. Some mornings I would drive Bobby to kindergarten on the back of my moped, and he loved it every time I did. He would grin from ear to ear the whole way to school. Then there were times when Sally would get on the back and we would go shopping around town. Having freedom brought some much needed joy into my life. It also made me feel really special that Dad would think of me so much that he would give me a gift out of the blue. Unfortunately, I never gave Mom Chase credit for this wonderful act. I think because Dad presented it without Mom, I never really connected the gift to her.

Instead of returning to the United States, I spent the next year bagging groceries at the commissary and taking whatever night classes I could. My heart wasn't into anything I did, and I didn't do very well in the college classes I was taking. I think I wound up dropping out of the shorthand class. I didn't know what direction to take my life or what I was supposed to do from there. It felt as if I was merely waiting for my adult life to just automatically start. DFCS never called to inquire about my life or to advise me of my choices at that point in life. I felt as if I was in a state of limbo. I was dating a GI at the time; and although I didn't love him, he was a nice guy and a good friend. We were part of a small international NATO base and the choices of single guys were VERY slim.

One day the sadness was more than I could handle, and I sat on the side of my bed with a handful of sleeping pills. Most of my friends had left and returned to the United States. Some came back to attend college and one came back to an engagement. As I looked at the handful of sleeping pills, I sat there missing the friends I had allowed into my heart. I remember asking God if this sadness was all there was to my life. I couldn't understand why He would bring me into the world to live a life like this. As I was debating the moment, I had an idea. I knew the guy I was dating wanted to marry me, and I decided that maybe this was my other out. So I decided to get married instead of taking the pills.

It wasn't long after that, that it was time for us to return to the United States. As we packed for our return to the United States, I mailed some of my belongings to California where I would be living with my husband after we married. It's rather funny now, but I mailed several wine glasses I had purchased at the Czechoslovakian border; and when I mailed them from Holland to California, I didn't wrap the glasses with anything. That's how naive I was and how much I had yet to learn. I was so NOT ready for marriage! I had major life skill inadequacies, severe social skill ineptness, and needed major mental and emotional repair before I gave myself to someone else. However, it was about survival, nothing more, merely survival. But, then, my entire life had been about survival....merely doing what it took to survive, yet another day.

9ᵗʰ Grade – Holland

THE ADULT YEARS

~~~~~~

"Smile despite the circumstances

and laugh throughout the pain.

Life is full of hardships,

but it is how you deal with them

that will, in the end,

define you."

Chapter 11

When we returned to the United States, I was really confused. We had left the State of South Carolina where I was a ward of the State, but I returned to Georgia. I didn't understand it but never questioned it either. Still, I never questioned anything. DFCS never called. I don't think they even knew we had returned to the United States, much less returned to a different state. I found this all very confusing. Where did I belong? Who did I belong to? What am I supposed to do next?

It would be another 2½ months before my fiancé returned to the United States from Holland. I was still 17 at the time and was living in the little town of Pooler with the Chase family. We were staying with Mom Chase's parents because Mom and Dad's house was still being built. Again, I felt very uncomfortable with the situation. I was extremely shy, and adjusting to new people was very hard for me. Mom Chase's brother, wife and baby girl were also living with them at the same time. Mom's brother and wife argued a lot, and I found that really uncomfortable and a little scary when they would yell at each other. Although it was always behind closed doors, you could hear it in the rest of the house. It reminded me of my dad and it scared me. I had been away from all of those memories for five years, and I couldn't bear being around it again. I was afraid the memories would come back and haunt me again. They frightened me.

So when my biological Aunt and Uncle wanted me to come for a visit, I thought it was perfect timing. I wasn't sure how I was going to get my driver's license or a job; so when my Aunt and Uncle contacted me from Warner Robins where I had lived as a little girl, I decided to go visit with them. It felt good to have "real" family. They seemed loving and very warm. I decided to stay with them until my fiancé returned to the United States. They drove me to Pooler to get the rest of my belongings. I think this hurt Mom's feelings. I didn't mean to do that, but I felt so uncomfortable staying there. I didn't see any way I could get a job or go to school living in a small town, and I dared not ask or talk about it. Pooler was a very small country town with very little job opportunities. So, I felt the best decision for me was to move to Warner Robins where I was much closer to opportunities; but I should have talked with Mom and told her how I felt. But I still didn't know how to communicate with anyone, and the fear that consumed me if I even thought about it was completely unbearable. Instead, I just did what I felt best without ever really saying or explaining anything. I wasn't comfortable talking to anyone about my feelings or what I was thinking, so I just kept everything all bottled up inside. It felt as if I was doing life all alone and everyday was spent merely trying to keep me together.

After moving to Warner Robins I realized that, without a driver's license, there still was not much opportunity for me to "start" my life. I had thought about not getting married; but without a car, no way to get a car, car insurance, or a job, there was little hope I could "start" my life without getting married. So once again, marriage won out. Although I really liked my Aunt and Uncle, I still felt out of place, uneasy, and scared. It was even harder to consider talking about my feelings there because I didn't know them. However, no one would have known how broken I was inside because I came across as jolly and happy about everything. The face I wore on the outside was not a true reflection of the broken soul that lived inside. I was trying to be what everyone wanted me to be. I just wanted to keep everyone happy, but I was failing miserably at it.

My fiancé returned to the United States somewhere around the beginning of June. My Aunt and Uncle had planned a small wedding in their front yard, and my future in-laws flew to Georgia to attend the wedding. We were married on June 14th in their front yard. I was 17 years old, three and one-half weeks before turning 18. Because I was underage, I had to have someone sign for me to get married.

Although my Aunt and Uncle were not my legal guardians, they signed for me to get married anyway.

No one talked to me about my options in life; no one reached out to help me plan a future. So what other option did I have? I was 17, I knew nothing about life; and when there is no one guiding you, there is no other option except to do what it takes to survive the only way you know how to survive. Foster children have major gaps in their life skill abilities, so skills that other teenagers have acquired by this age are skills that foster children have no knowledge of, as was the case with me.

Tim and I married and we moved to Escalon, California. We stayed at Tim's parents' house until we found an apartment. Tim decided not to reenlist in the Army and had decided to take over the family farm instead. When Tim and I moved into our first apartment, we had very few belongings since we were newlyweds. Tim's family gathered together an apartment full of furniture and household items necessary to start a home. They did such a wonderful job, that we only had a few things we had to buy.

Tim's family was a large Italian family, and they hosted a wedding reception for us. I found all of the attention very uncomfortable. I wasn't used to family, much less a large Italian family. However, it was nice receiving gifts and household items that we needed. I don't remember looking very many people in the eye that day; I was still very shy and lacked any spark of self-confidence or self-esteem. I found this gathering socially painful and couldn't wait to get home.

We started attending the same church Tim's mother attended, and we became part of the weekly congregation. We immediately joined a couples' Bible study and were enjoying life as a newly married couple. I still didn't have my driver's license, but I was offered a job as a receptionist at a clinical laboratory where the preacher's wife worked. She came by to pick me up every morning, and I really enjoyed working with her. This job opportunity helped with my self-confidence issues. I still had a long way to go, but I felt a little better about myself. My next step was to start driving and possibly start some college classes.

Several weeks later I came down with the flu and missed several days of work. We started getting a little worried, so we thought I had better go to the doctor. While I was in the doctor's office, the doctor came into the room and asked if I was using any birth control. I looked at him and said, "No." He looked at me as if I was the most stupid woman he had ever seen. I knew you could get pregnant, and I knew how it happened -- but that was pretty much all I knew about it. No one had ever talked to me about birth control and how easy it truly is to get pregnant. I know it sounds rather silly, but I never really thought about pregnancy while I was married. Maybe I was in such a fog because of all the change I was facing, but it never crossed my mind. No one ever said, "Helen, you are about to get married. Do you want a baby right away? If not, then maybe you should go and visit the doctor and get birth control pills." I felt so stupid that day. Needless to say the "flu" continued for another 2½ months, and I no longer had the job I enjoyed so much.

On April 21, 1981, a beautiful baby girl named Tanya Michelle was born. As they laid that beautiful baby in my arms, I fell in love for the very first time in my life. This beautiful little girl weighed 6lb. 3ozs. and was 18½ inches long. I told her, "Hello," smiled at her and then immediately went to sleep cuddling my beautiful baby in my arms. I don't even remember them taking her out of my arms. They delivered her by cesarean section, so I was still very groggy at the time. She was the prettiest baby I had ever seen. My life began the day I gave birth to my beautiful baby girl. I vowed to God that she would never live the life I lived. I vowed to Him that I would be the best mom I could be. I loved this little bundle more than words could say. She filled that deep, dark pit in my heart and it suddenly came alive. Although I still had been living in a numb emotional state, something happened the moment they put that beautiful baby in my arms.

Life continued busily with a new baby in tow, and I loved every minute of it. Tanya was a very happy baby and hardly ever cried. When she was about three months old, I decided to get my driver's license. By then I was 19 years old. The first time I took the test I failed. I forgot to look behind me when I backed up. I only looked in my rearview mirror, and the instructor stopped the test 2 minutes after we started, immediately failing me. This was quite a blow, but I quickly recovered. The second time I took my test, I passed. It felt good to be a little more independent.

During one of my first trips driving, I had to drive over a railroad track. We had a car with a manual transmission at the time and I was driving over the track when the car suddenly stopped. When the car stopped, it was straddling the tracks and wouldn't start or back up. It wouldn't move; it just sat right there no matter what I did. All of a sudden, I heard a very loud whistle. It was coming from a train that was close and moving fast. When I looked up, all I could see was a very large, bright round light coming very quickly in my direction. I tried stepping on the clutch, but still the car wouldn't move. I could feel the rumbling of the tracks as the train neared our car. At this point, all I could think about was the baby strapped securely in the back seat and how close this train was. As I quickly assessed our options, I knew Tim and I could get out of the car safely; but we would have to leave the baby behind. There was no time to get her out of the car seat before the train hit the car. My hands were gripped tightly on the steering wheel. I didn't say a word and neither did Tim. I didn't know what to do. All of a sudden as the train was upon us, I saw Tim put his hand on the door handle getting ready to jump out. In a very calm voice, I looked at him and said, "Don't you dare get out of this car! If one goes, we all go." Tim took his hand off the door handle, and we silently decided to die together that day. Once I made the decision to die with my family, a calmness came over me. I remember saying a quick prayer, I closed my eyes and I clutched the steering wheel preparing to meet my Father that day. All of a sudden, the car moved backwards off of the train tracks. I didn't see anything because my eyes were closed, but the car moved backwards off of the train tracks all by itself. Although the car moved off the tracks, we were still so close to the train that you could feel the car move to the right as the train sped by. My eyes were still closed, but I could feel our car move to the right from the force of the air generated by the train. With my eyes closed, it felt as if I could reach my hand out and touch the train as it passed by.

Once the train passed, I quietly opened my door and ever so slowly made my way to the other side of the car. My legs were so wobbly that I literally had to hold onto the car to walk to the other side without falling down. I was scared to death. I was a little angry now because it dawned on me that we had had a problem with the battery wire jumping off the terminal, and I knew what had probably just happened. Tim got out and opened the hood, put the wire back on the battery terminal and drove us home. We never spoke about the incident -- we were just thankful to be alive. I can truly say that I love my child so much that I know beyond a shadow of a doubt that I would die for her. It seemed as if God was asking me that question; and once I answered it, he spared our lives. That's the way I like to think about it, anyway.

Although I was now a mother, I still felt the desire to do something more. I needed to go back to school or work. I needed to find "me." I still felt lost inside; I still didn't know where I belonged. Tim's family was nice, but they had a different kind of relationship. They weren't that all-American, warm and fuzzy, all-about-family kind of family. There seemed to be a lot of disconnect within their family unit, and it wasn't the family environment I had imagined my family would be. However, I absolutely loved being a mother and I couldn't get enough of my beautiful baby girl.

Tim and I got along okay; but like most married couples, we began seeing each other's negatives. I was a clean freak and Tim was quite the opposite. I was phenomenal with finances, but Tim . . . not quite so much. I was a perfectionist and expected a lot out of all of us, especially myself. I needed to work or go to school. I needed more in my life because I still needed to be constantly busy to chase the away the bad memories. The floors in the apartment were clean enough to eat off, the windows glistened and the toilets were immaculate; but I needed more to my life than just being a mother and a housewife.

When Tanya was 6 months old, I decided to visit Georgia and share my new baby with Mom and Dad Chase. I also wanted a break from my husband. We did everything together and I needed some space, some "me time." I was beginning to feel very smothered. I needed to talk to Mom about this displacement that I still felt in my heart. I thought that now that I'm a wife and mother, maybe Mom and I could have a better relationship. When Tim's family found out that I was going to Georgia, they decided to surprise me and buy a ticket for him so he could go with me. They said we were never apart and that they thought I would be lost without him. Little did they know I felt I needed some breathing room. They meant well, but I wish they would have asked first.

I didn't return to California with Tim that trip; I stayed there with Mom and Dad Chase. They had finished their new house and had room for me and Tanya to spend some time there to figure out what I wanted in life. It worked for a little while, but I still felt out of place for some reason. I didn't have any friends there, and I couldn't get a job. So, after a few months, I returned to California with Tim. I didn't feel I belonged anywhere. I was emotionally lost and I still couldn't find the path to my future. After a few months in California again, I decided to move back to Georgia for good. I never felt at home in California, and I wanted to be close to my sister and what "family" I had.

My family consisted of Mom and Dad Chase and my Aunt and Uncle in Warner Robins; however, they were not friends with each other so that made the "family" situation a little difficult. No matter where I stayed, the other was hurt and I didn't want to hurt anyone. However, Mom Chase never talked badly about my Aunt and Uncle, but my Aunt and Uncle made it clear how they felt about the Chases. My real family never appreciated what the Chases did for us. We weren't their family, yet they opened their hearts and their home to us. They kept us safe after my family threw us away. Were there problems when I lived with the Chases? Absolutely. But I was a teenager and, as adults, my Aunt and Uncle should have pointed that the issues I was having at with the Chase's were mostly normal teenage issues instead of fueling the fire. They needed to tell me what I needed to hear, not what I wanted to hear.

I finally decided to move to Warner Robins where the job opportunities were much better. I kept family persuasion out of the mix and made a decision based on what was best for me and my child. I wanted to stay with Mom and Dad Chase, but they didn't live where jobs were close and plentiful. Although Mom and I didn't always see eye to eye, we knew each other and I felt comfortable with our relationship. Our relationship was actually much better. I also knew that our relationship was real, and that was something I could live with. I always felt that my relationship with my biological Aunt and Uncle was conditional; it didn't always feel real. Maybe it was because I didn't know them well enough. There was always something uneasy about my biological family. I still don't understand it, but it exists to this day. Their relationship always felt conditional and a little fake, but I knew they were trying. It sounds odd, but my only real relationship was that which I shared with my foster family. To me, it felt as if I was a baby bird who fell out of its nest; and because another mother touched me and had their scent on me, I was no longer completely acceptable by my biological family, that in their eyes I would forever be tainted and damaged. It felt as if I was now "Nobody's Child."

During these next few years, I remained in Warner Robins. I started working as a waitress at the officers' club and went to school during the day. Then I was offered a job at the Holiday Inn where I worked at the front desk and eventually became the part-time weekend auditor as well. I continued to take computer classes and became a major player in the training of our staff when we switched from a manual system over to a new computer system at the Holiday Inn. My Aunt and Uncle babysat Tanya while I worked. Eventually, I started working as a bookkeeper during the day at the corporate office of a daycare center. Tanya started attending daycare during the day when I worked for the daycare center, and my Aunt and Uncle kept her when I worked evenings and weekends at the Holiday Inn.

During this time Tanya started calling my Aunt and Uncle, Granddaddy and Grandmamma and referred to Mom and Dad Chase as Granny and Papa Chase. I made trips as often as I could to Mom and Dad's. I wanted them to know that, although I lived in Warner Robins, they were still my family and a very big part of my life. I was still very quiet and didn't really share much with anyone, so it was easy for people to feel left out of my life. I was happy with Tanya calling my Aunt and Uncle Grandmamma and Granddaddy because I knew this was the only biological family environment I could provide for her and wanted her to have a different family life than I had. Also, I felt they had earned that privilege. I thought I was doing what was best for her, especially since Tim and I were divorced and his family lived far away. Once again, I felt this was as good as it gets for someone like me.

Chapter 12

I didn't like dating and I was never really good at it. I hardly talked, had no self-confidence or self-esteem. I didn't think I was pretty and thought I was way too thin. I kept asking God, "How do you know if a guy loves you if you've never known love before -- except the love of a child, which is a very different kind of love?"

It's actually kind of funny how I met Clark. My sister, Vicky, wanted me to go to a bar with her; and since I had never ever been to a bar before, I wouldn't go unless I had a male escort. I wasn't a partier; I was a mother first and foremost. So a friend of hers came along and there we went. Again, the first guy in my life, and I wind up in a relationship thinking this is a good as it gets for someone like me. I also lacked any skill about dating and found dating socially painful; so, this kept me from having to date. I was incredibly shy, lacked any self-confidence, had no self-esteem and really didn't think very highly of myself -- all the skills one needs to possess in order to date. How do you know when you're in love if you can't even feel your own heart? How can you trust a man you don't know if you can't even trust your own family? I was in no condition to be finding the man I was supposed to spend the rest of my life with and lacked the resources and time to do anything about it.

During my relationship with Clark, my oldest sister, Dottie, moved to Warner Robins and I was beyond elated. I was so happy to have the opportunity to know her again. I know this must sound strange for someone from an ordinary family; but for foster children, this scenario is far too common. I had missed her so much! I felt this was the start of something wonderful for me for a change.

Dottie had a son from a previous marriage. He was such a sweet little boy and she loved him so much. I didn't care very much for Dottie's husband, though. He was a drug addict, beat her, ran around on her and didn't like to work.

Since I worked at the Holiday Inn, I got Dottie a job as a waitress; but that didn't last very long. So then I got her a job as a cook at one of the daycare centers with the other company I worked for. She started working at the same daycare center where Tanya stayed and she seemed to like her job. She would often take Tanya out for ice cream after her lunch shift, and Tanya loved spending time with her Aunt Dottie. Tanya talked about Dottie often and how much she loved her. It felt really good having a sister in my life with whom I could share a normal sibling relationship. Finally, I had family that I completely loved, trusted and adored. I needed this relationship so terribly bad.

Dottie and I got to know each other again. With working two jobs and a child, we didn't get to see each other as much as I would have liked, so I treasured every moment we were together. During our visits together, Dottie would tell me stories of our life when mother was alive. She spoke of a day when Dad locked our mother in the refrigerator. Dottie said Dad threw all of the food out of the refrigerator, took out the shelves and stuffed Mom inside. Then he put a chair in front to wedge against the latch to keep it from opening. Thankfully, a neighbor came by and found her while she was still alive. Dottie said she had tried to move the chair herself, but it was wedged so tightly she couldn't budge it without help.

She spoke of a day when Dad came in drunk and angry. She said Danny was crying and it made Dad so angry that he picked him up and threw him across the room against the wall. She looked at me with tears in her eyes and said, "He threw him so hard, Helen, I thought he was dead. He laid there lifeless in a heap at the bottom of the wall and, then all of a sudden, he started crying." The way she spoke, the impact must have knocked him out. Danny must have been just a toddler at the time.

She spoke of so much pain, so much misery. I hated to ask anything; you could tell it was painful for her to speak of these events. I thought, "Do I really want to know all of this?"; but I knew I needed to hear it. I needed to know what they went through. I needed to feel my mother's pain. I thought, "I won't ask questions. I will just quietly absorb the information as she feels comfortable enough to go deeper, deeper into her mind and deeper into her heart. I won't push, we have the rest of our lives. This time I won't lose her and, in time, she will open up completely, slowly. In time, I will know everything there is to know about our past."

Dottie spoke of a day when Mom was pregnant and Dad pushed her down the stairs causing her to lose the baby. Dottie also said that wasn't Mom's first miscarriage by our father's hands either. Dottie said the violence got so bad that Mom took us four children to Oregon to live with Mom's brother. I used to have a picture of us kids and my cousins together in Oregon in my photo album . . . until I had a visitor and it disappeared.

Dottie said Mother and I had a very close relationship, me being just a baby at the time. She spoke of times when Mom would play with me. Dottie told me Mother had made a pillow for me and that I carried it everywhere I went. She said I slept with it every night. Dottie said when we went to Oregon, somehow it got lost and I couldn't sleep. She said I just cried and wouldn't stop crying, so Mom had to make me another one so I could sleep.

Dottie said when we lived in Oregon, our mother worked as a cocktail waitress; and one day while mother was working, I started crying and wouldn't stop. She said that I was still in a crib at the time and that she would put her hands through the bars to feed me because she wasn't tall enough to reach in and pick me up. According to Dottie, I was a very good baby and only cried when I was hungry or needed a diaper changed. She said that on this particular night I wouldn't stop crying, which was quite unusual, and that she couldn't get me to stop. Since she couldn't get me out of the crib, she went downstairs and outside to find Mother. Dottie said she was very scared because it was pretty dark and not a very good place to be at night. She said someone reached out and touched her on the back of the arm, and it scared her so badly that she passed out. Dottie said it was Mom and that Mom felt horrible for scaring her that badly. Dottie understood that she had to help with us so Mom could work and said she was glad to do it because that meant Dad wasn't around.

The way it sounded, I think Dottie must have taken care of us a lot. Dottie said that Dad came to Oregon and forced Mom to move back to South Carolina with him. Dottie said he physically and violently made her go back to him. *He made her* go back to a life of horror. She also said that things got even more violent after we moved back.

It was then that I asked Dottie about something I dreamt about often. I told her that I remember us being really scared and hiding behind a chair in the living room. I remembered seeing a man's face in the window of the front door. She said that a man had tried to break into our house and that we were really scared. She said that it was during the time that Mom was having really bad headaches and wasn't able to get out of bed. She said Mom was in her room in bed and couldn't do anything to protect us. Dottie said the man finally left. I was so glad that I finally did remember something from when Mom was alive. I was hoping in time I would remember something about my Mom.

I told Dottie I remembered eating a lot of beans. She said that we ate Pork n' Beans and half of a hot dog for dinner every night but that Fridays were special because we got to split a candy bar as well. She said we would take one candy bar and cut it into fourths and share it. Dottie said that Mom was so sick that she had to make our dinner and that was all she could cook. She said Mom was often in a lot of pain because of her headaches.

Those were the only two things I could remember from when Mom was alive. I so desperately wanted to remember something about my Mom, but I never could.

I finally worked up the courage to ask Dottie why she left after coming to live with Dad and Glenda. She said that Glenda walked in on Dad doing things to her that fathers don't do with daughters.

She said that it caused tension between her and Glenda and that they thought it best that she left. She also said that Glenda blamed her for it. I was taken aback when I heard that. I was so sad to hear that Glenda would blame Dottie for something like that. I knew the kind of man my dad was and never would have doubted what she had just said and wondered how Glenda could have sided with my dad.

I was finally getting the courage and felt comfortable enough to ask Dottie questions. I thought, "I'll just leave it with this one question. I don't want to push it too much. I'll ask her more later, there's always tomorrow."

It felt so good to finally have that sister relationship that normal sisters have. I was never able to have that with my other sister, Vicky; so it felt really good to know that I was lovable as a sister. Dottie and I talked every day; I would put the telephone in my pocket and we talked for hours while I cleaned house. This felt really good because I was never able to share that much of me with anyone before. I was never that confident in having conversations like that. I was so amazed at how easily it flowed. I didn't struggle with it . . . it just flowed all on its own.

I didn't get to hear any more stories from my sister. This beautiful woman left my life as quickly as she came into it. On December 18, 1985, my sister, Dorothy Shumpert, went to live in heaven with my mother. At the young age of 31, this amazing woman was blown from the back of a truck, and she died of massive head injuries. I thought we had forever, but I quickly found that life is precious and life is often very short. This wonderful sister of mine was only on this earth for 31 short, mostly violent years. She died never really knowing much happiness, never really knowing what "real" family was all about. I loved my sister inside and out, but her life was not the life that she needed to have been living. Her life was so sad, and I tried desperately to help her. She had to leave her husband in order to help herself, but she couldn't bring herself to do that. I begged her to bring her little boy, Brian, and come live with me . . . but she wouldn't.

I was annoyed with Dottie the day she died. She was supposed to watch Tanya while I went to work. I saw her a few weeks prior, and she said she wanted to spend time with Tanya and take her out for ice cream. When I stopped by to drop Tanya off she wasn't there, so I took her to my Aunt and Uncle's. Her telephone had been disconnected so I couldn't call her to remind her, and I didn't want to stop by because I was looking a little "fluffy." I was pregnant and didn't quite know how to tell Dottie. She had been trying to get pregnant for years; and although she didn't need a baby with her current husband, she desperately wanted to give him one. I wasn't sure how she was going to take the news of my pregnancy, so I was avoiding her so I wouldn't have to tell her. If only I had reminded her.........

I didn't cry the day they buried my sister. I knew she was in a much happier place. She was with the one person she loved most, our mother. If I could change anything, it would have been that I had taken the day off from work and been there when that beautiful lady left this earth. Her husband had called me and told me they were going to take her off life support; however, I had decided it was more important to go to work. There was a very important meeting that day on the new computer system we were installing. We were about to go live and I was on the training team. My Uncle in Warner Robins also called and encouraged me not to come to the hospital. However, if I could do this one event over today, I would choose to be with my sister when she took her last breath. If I had that day to do over again, I would have been holding that beautiful lady's hand when God took her home. But I didn't have the heart that I have today. Today I feel *everything* and today I would have been there for her. Some days I miss her so much it hurts. I miss that beautiful smile and those sparkling eyes so much. Someday I will understand why.... why our lives were so full of pain and heartache. Were we cursed? Again, I couldn't understand how God could allow so much pain and misery happen to one family. The one comforting thought I had was that she was in a much better place. She was with Mom and she loved Mom so much. I didn't get to learn everything about my life, but maybe God felt it was all I could handle.

Chapter 13

Clark and I married about four weeks before Dottie passed away. Clark didn't want any more children, but I did. We had lived together for a couple of years and had actually gone our separate ways for awhile because that was something I felt strongly about, and it was a deal breaker for me. Clark compromised on having a baby but said I had to get pregnant immediately. He was about to turn 30 and he didn't want children after 30. I wanted to wait a couple of years because I didn't want to start a new marriage with a new baby as I did before, but I compromised and made plans to get pregnant as soon as possible. I knew I only had one chance for a baby boy so I did all the research I could to maximize the possibilities of conceiving a boy. We were married on November 14, 1985; and nine months later on August 22, 1986, they laid a beautiful baby boy in my arms. Christopher Mark weighed 7lbs. 11½ozs. and was 22½ inches long.

About four months into my pregnancy, Clark was laid off from his job. He had been there for many years, so we were both pretty surprised and devastated over the news. I had painstakingly planned out every little detail of this new journey. I had just finished paying off our car and was putting money in the bank so I could stay home for six months. I wanted to enjoy this new baby and spend time with Tanya as a stay-at-home mother for a little while. I had already made one mistake with my carefully planned calculations because I had scheduled my C-section the same day Tanya started kindergarten. I had everything planned out so well that I even calculated two days off from work to spend with Tanya before going to the hospital. But I never could have imagined having to make room for complications such as this to my carefully made plans.

During the last part of my pregnancy, Clark lived in Atlanta training with Lockheed Martin in Marietta, Georgia. When Christopher turned 6 weeks old, we moved to a suburb of Atlanta. After we found a house to rent and settled in, I started looking for a job. I really liked the job market in the Atlanta area and decided I really liked living there. It didn't take long to find a job, and I started working as a bookkeeper for a small embroidery company. The pay in the Atlanta area was much better than the Warner Robins area and jobs were much more plentiful. I found this to actually be a blessing in disguise. I always felt a little guilty for living in Warner Robins, anyway. Although Mom never said anything derogatory about my living there, I *felt* like it meant I was choosing sides but I wasn't. So moving to the Atlanta area actually took a weight off of my shoulders that had been there for a long time. It also felt as if my family in Warner Robins was trying to take more of a parental role with Tanya instead of a grandparent role, so the distance was good to help balance that part of my family life.

Christopher was a very healthy baby but suffered from frequent ear infections, and Tanya was suffering from frequent bouts of tonsillitis. So, life was very busy with work and doctor visits. During my six month follow-up after giving birth to Christopher, the doctor was concerned and did further testing. I was informed that I was in the beginning stages of cancer. For the next several months, life was a juggling act of work, sick children and constant treatments for me. The doctors decided that something had to give and I couldn't continue battling all that I was battling. It was starting to take a toll on my health. Clark started work very early and came home early which made it possible for him to take on a part-time job to carry us through until my health scare was over and I could go back to work. However, Clark said he worked to live and didn't live to work. So I was saddled with juggling two sick children, working 40+ hours a week and had to fit in medical procedures whenever I could for the cancer. Every long weekend and holiday was now spent with some type of a procedure I had to have, hoping this would be "the one" that worked.

The doctors decided that the first thing we needed to do was to have Tanya's tonsils taken out, and then we put Christopher on a low dose antibiotic for a year to help with the ear infections. This took care of the kids so I could concentrate on my health and my job. I had no choice but to work through the cancer because we needed my income. Clark kept getting laid off at Lockheed and couldn't/ wouldn't find stable employment. This is also when I found out that Clark had a drug problem. Clark and I had always worked opposite shifts and really didn't see each other often, so this gave him a lot of time without me around. During this time, he obviously had a life I knew nothing about. We always had a shed everywhere we lived, but I never put two and two together. Clark loved to tinker with stuff in his shed, and I was busy cleaning when I wasn't working. So it all worked out and I never questioned why I didn't have a key to the shed. I never went out there unless he was there, so it really didn't matter to me and I never thought anything of it. Maybe the signs were there and I didn't want to see them? Either way, I was completely oblivious to everything that was going on. Was I too busy to see it; did I close my eyes to it; or did I truly not see the obvious? I don't know. To me, it was merely a shed where he tinkered with stuff.

I tried to find Mom to talk with her about everything that was going on but found that Mom and Dad Chase were in the process of a nasty divorce. I lost them. I had no idea where they were or how to get in touch with them. It would be many years before I found them again.

I continued to work all throughout my bout with cancer. As I was nearing the end of illness, I noticed Clark coming from Tanya's room in the middle of the night with only his underwear on. I questioned him, and in the morning I talked with Tanya as well. I informed Clark that this would never happen again. I also informed him that his marriage was on the line. What seemed so odd is that Clark was never around Tanya in "just" his underwear, so why would this happen in the middle of the night? Everyone assured me all was fine and nothing was happening, yet there was a sick feeling in the pit of my stomach. I wasn't going to take *any chances* with my daughter. I made my position completely clear with Clark before the conversation was over.

A few weeks later, I saw Clark coming from Tanya's room in the middle of the night wearing only his underwear again. I decided that that was it. As soon as the doctors released me, I was leaving. Clark spent most of his free time in the shed with his drugs anyway. I felt I had no choice but to take my children and provide a safe environment for them.

The day the doctor released me from care, I started making plans. I was already saving money and had found an apartment close to Tanya's school so she could continue life without many changes. However, after talking with my Aunt and Uncle, we decided it would be best if Tanya finished the school year with them in Warner Robins. We were afraid that Clark would blame the divorce on Tanya and might even try to hurt her. So, with a very heavy heart I decided to do what was best for my child, to keep her out of the middle and keep her safe. I was probably over-protecting her, but I felt it was necessary. I could never have made it through losing a child, especially if it were my fault. So my Aunt and Uncle convinced me I was doing the right thing and the best thing for my daughter. What scared me was that it felt as if they wanted Tanya for themselves. I had an eerie feeling about this but shook it off as me being unable to trust anyone.

I made plans to leave on a day when my Aunt and Uncle could be there to pick up Tanya and keep me safe should that become an issue. I had taken the day off to pack up whatever we needed and leave. So after Clark left for work, I did exactly that. I hired movers to do the heavy work. We worked very quickly and it wasn't long before it was completed. Clark had no idea I was leaving or where I was going. I left him the house and a car we were purchasing. I knew he wouldn't sign it over to me, so I took cash and bought a cheap used car. I didn't want to fight about it . . . I just wanted out. It got ugly and I was glad that Tanya wasn't there to be brought into the middle. But when my Aunt spoke of a Mother's Day gift Tanya had made at school and had given to her, I started wondering about the decision I had made and the paper they encouraged me to sign.

I found out that my Aunt and Uncle had taken Tanya to the Ronald McDonald House to be sure she wasn't molested. I'm glad they did that, but I think they should have talked to me before making a decision like that on their own. After all, I was her mother and should have been informed about any major decisions concerning *my* child. Although verification was a relief, she had already been to a doctor to verify the same. My Aunt and Uncle were beginning to take on a parental role, and I was slowly being pushed out. I had signed a custody paper my Uncle typed up so they could enroll her in school and seek medical attention, but I never thought about it not having an expiration date or the exact wording in the document. After all, they were family and would keep my best interest at heart . . . *or would they?* I had so much going on and I was trying to do what was best for my child, and I made the mistake of trusting someone. I made the mistake of trusting family. The one time I had allowed myself to trust someone would be the biggest mistake of my life.

Tanya was an excellent student. I had taught her to read by the time she was 3 years old. She excelled at almost everything she did, and everyone loved being around her. I finally got Tanya back after about 6 months, but things would never be the same. My Aunt and Uncle kept getting into the middle of our relationship. They felt I was a bad mother and that they could parent her better than I could. They would call her when I wasn't home to find out the "scoop," and they often talked negatively about me to her behind my back. I finally put the telephones on a switch where I could turn them off when I wasn't home. This made them VERY angry and it began a full-blown war between us. They decided they were going to have her back one way or another. I didn't drink, I didn't party, I didn't do drugs, I worked and I had to work a lot; but my children were well taken care of. They participated in after-school activities, their grades were excellent, they often won awards and were very well behaved. I was often exhausted and wasn't always extremely patient. I didn't always parent the way my family thought I should parent, but I didn't agree with the way they thought I should parent and didn't agree with the way they parented their children, either.

Dottie told me some not so pretty stories from when she lived with them. She never spoke of many good times. My ex-in-laws had no qualms with the way I parented, nor did anyone else I knew. My

Aunt tried to talk my ex-in-laws into taking custody of Christopher. My ex-mother-in-law saw me and told me what was going on and said they thought I had been a great mother and didn't deserve what was happening with Tanya. I never understood what was so bad about my parenting. No two people parent alike; and considering my childhood, I think I was doing an excellent job. Who were *they* to judge me, anyway; and, more importantly, after knowing what I had been through, how could they add more pain and sorrow to my life? They hurt me worse than anyone in my life could have and they were supposed to be my family. They even said they loved me, but their actions told the truth.

What fueled this fight even more was that, during my marriage with Clark, my father came into the picture. He wanted to know his grandchildren and I allowed him the opportunity. My Aunt and Uncle were appalled that I would even consider allowing this. My Uncle had written his family off years ago. However, my dad had stopped drinking and was not the violent man he had been. I prayed really hard about it and thought it was the right thing to do. I was supposed to forgive and that I could do, but I knew I would never be able to forget. He visited with his wife and my half-sister and things went well, but my Uncle was furious with me.

Shortly after I divorced Clark, I met a guy who fell head over heels in love with me and we eventually moved in together. I was now much closer to my job and could spend more time with my children. He had a wonderful family and they accepted us with open arms. With the way his family treated us, you would have thought my children were his biological children and we all became very close. His mother was in our lives almost daily. They spent holidays with us and took us on family vacations -- our first ever vacations -- and they loved us unconditionally. Time went on and he demanded that I either marry him or move out. I wasn't prepared to move out. I needed more time to save up and to prepare my children, so I agreed to marry him. Again, the very first guy after my divorce and here I go again. As the wedding date approached, my feet grew colder and colder. I had waited so long to order the invitations that I had to rush them in, but then I couldn't bring myself to mail them out. I wasn't ready to marry again. I needed to put myself back together first, and I couldn't do that while being in a constant battle with my daughter and my Aunt and Uncle. I loved this relationship, but there were issues we needed to work on; and I think I was more in love with the idea of this wonderful family I had never had than I was with him. I knew I didn't want to repeat a mistake I was commonly known for: jumping into a marriage I wasn't sure would last a lifetime. I started questioning my judgment and knew I needed to change so much about myself first. I wanted to break this cycle I was in, and the first thing I decided I needed to do was to make better decisions. I didn't know how I was going to do this, but I knew I definitely needed to start by making better decisions. I remember asking God, "How do you know if a decision is a good decision if you don't find out whether it was good or bad until years later?" I was so confused about how to know if a decision was good or bad before you made it. I was never taught about decision making. I found this very confusing and it was such an important skill to have. Although I must have been about 28 or 29 years old at this time, I still had the life skills of a teenager.

So, I moved out and I told myself I would never live with a guy ever again. There was just too much hurt for everyone, especially the children. In fact, I decided I wouldn't allow my children to get close to any man again until it became extremely serious. For the first time in my life I was financially able to survive on my own. This was huge for me. I had completed task #1 – financially able to survive on my own. Now on to task #2 – learning to make good decisions.

Chapter 14

There I was, on my own again; but this time it was going to be different. This time I told myself, "I'm going to find time for me." It was time to learn the life skills I was in desperate need of, to fill countless gaps in my social skill abilities and try to make me complete once and for all. With so many holes, so little time and absolutely no tools, how do I get started?

Shortly after I moved out and was on my own, I thought I would start my new life by making my first good decision. I started dating a Christian man. His name was JR. I thought, "Wow, what a great decision! I'm dating a Christian man." Then I looked up to heaven and said, "God, I just know you've got to be happy about this. I'm finally dating a Christian man. Aren't you proud of me?" He was very nice, very attentive, smart, and decisive. He owned the company I worked for, and he was married. I know . . . looking back at it, how was that a good decision? But, at that time in my life, I think I thought this was a safe decision because obviously marriage would never be an issue and living together would never be an issue either. I worked with his wife all the time, and she had said on a couple of occasions that she didn't care what he did as long as he didn't touch her and took care of her financially. Not in those exact words, but I understood the gist of it. No, I'm not proud of myself; but they obviously had a different type of marriage. I also worked so much that I didn't have time to date, so this arrangement was very convenient and I was learning a lot from him.

My dad and step-mother came to visit a couple of times with my half-sister after Clark and I were divorced. One weekend I had to go out of town on business, and the couple I typically paid to babysit wasn't available. So my dad, Betty and my half-sister came to watch the kids while I was gone. My half-sister said she would sleep in the same bedroom as my daughter, so I felt safe with that. My dad was still not drinking anymore due to health problems so violence was no longer an issue. However, after I returned from my trip, I was told that Christopher wasn't in a good mood one morning so my dad popped him on the head and called him a vulgar name. He didn't hit him hard enough to hurt him, but calling my child names like that was unacceptable. So that was the last time I ever saw my dad. I felt that after all the pain and tragedy he caused in my life, he was very lucky to have had that opportunity. I felt that what he did was completely unacceptable and showed me that life was still "all about him." But allowing my father to babysit my children was the ultimate sin to my Uncle. He vowed to take Tanya away from me no matter what it took. He said this showed how unfit of a parent I truly was. I felt I had a responsibility to my children, to myself and to my Lord to forgive and give my father a chance to prove himself. I think my Uncle felt I was betraying him; but he wasn't my father -- he was my Uncle. And although I allowed my child to call him Granddaddy, he was in fact not her Granddaddy. However, I had no intentions of taking that title from him merely because she was calling my father Granddaddy as well.

I worked hard and still had to work a lot, but I didn't party or anything. I just worked extremely hard to provide for my family on my own. My favorite place to be if I wasn't working was at home with my children, taking them to their activities or to church on Sundays. Things with Tanya went from bad to worse, and she wanted to live with my Aunt and Uncle. In the State of Georgia, a child 12 years and above can choose who they want to live with as long as it is an immediate family member. However, in a normal family environment, parents have a love for their children that isn't present in outside relationships. But, because I had allowed them to take a grandparent role, it helped their case of being deemed immediate family. The judge also took into account the fact that I, too, had lived with them when I was a child and cited that I had been raised in the foster system. Again, the label I wore followed me into court. I didn't beat or abuse my children in any way whatsoever. Occasionally

I'm impatient, but I'm human like every other parent in the world. It didn't help that I had signed a custody paper with no expiration date, either.

Tanya went to live with my Aunt and Uncle . . . and I was heartbroken. I broke down in court; and when we left, my Uncle had the guts to say, "That was a nice show you put on in there." I just looked at him; he obviously knew nothing of my heart. To be honest, deep down inside I knew she had to live with them to realize what she was really getting into. They had already made their mark on her heart, and she needed to find out reality on her own. Otherwise, at the next argument, she would wonder what it could have been like if she had gone to live with them and it would have become a forever battle. So, with a heavy heart, I let her go; but I made it clear I would always be there for her no matter what.

It didn't last long before they started having the same trouble with Tanya as I had been having, and they kicked her out. They wouldn't bring her to me; instead, they took her to live with her dad. I didn't want that because I knew he had no rules; and I knew it would be impossible for her to go from no rules back into my home with rules. And, as I figured, Tanya loved living with her dad. He had no rules. Again, that didn't last very long before he told her she had to find someplace else to live because he was broke. He had spent all of his money trying to buy her while she was still living with me.

Tanya knew she could come back and live with me any time she wanted, the only stipulation was that she had to abide by my rules. Her father had no rules for her, and she didn't feel she could live with my rules, so she lived on her own at 16. My Aunt, my Uncle and her father gave her an easy out; and as any teenage child would, she took it. It broke my heart to have my baby girl go through what she did, pain caused by grown adults who knew better. They may have judged me, but it's not my place to judge them. God will judge them one day, and it's His place to do so. Tanya was merely a child being a child, doing what children do best -- anything to get what they want at the moment . . . Or what they think they want at the moment, anyway. The only things I did in my life that were wrong were living with a guy without marriage and dating a married guy. Not good decisions, but survival nonetheless. I cried everyday for a very long time. There was a hole in my heart for many years. It tore me up not to have my baby girl in my arms every day. I made sure they never had the opportunity to build a relationship with my son.

There came a time when JR, the married guy I was seeing, became ill; and I had no choice but to take over the company responsibilities. I didn't mind running the company; I learned more than I could ever have imagined and loved absorbing everything I could. JR had a terrible problem with kidney stones and was in and out of the hospital often. By this time, we had been seeing each other for about 9 years. I now worked mainly from home and spent a lot of time at locations, sales calls or corporate attorney visits.

We spent a lot of time with JR's family. His parents and sisters accepted me as if I were his wife. They actually spent far more time with him and I than they did with him and his family. I think he was beginning to forget which woman he was married to and was becoming a very jealous man. I gave him absolutely no reason to be jealous, but his jealousy was turning into obsession and it was starting to scare me. The first 8 years of our relationship was awesome; we had an incredible life together. The business was growing by leaps and bounds. We were actually dubbed the dynamic duo by other business people. A television channel even spotlighted us in a business review they were doing. We were kicking booty and taking names! I loved it. I found the self-confidence and self-esteem I had never known. I felt wonderful about myself. This was new and exciting. I grew in ways I never thought possible. We had fun; we worked and laughed all the time. I learned so much from this amazing man. I was able to talk about anything and everything. I no longer struggled with words, self-esteem or self-confidence. We had tons of fun no matter what we were doing. We went for sushi and I told him the green stuff was avocado. He ate it in one bite; and with tears running down his face, we both laughed until we cried. After eating Indian food, as we walked outside, I tripped him, not meaning for him to fall. But fall he did; and with a hole in his suit pants and a bloody knee, we both laughed once again until we cried. We had a fabulous relationship and nothing was off limits. We did everything together; I trusted this man with my heart and with my life. For the first time ever, I gave everything I had to someone else and this man adored everything about me. He wined and dined me; he brought me flowers and showered me with gifts. He took Christopher and me on vacations and we had wonderful times. He would bring his son over to play with Christopher, and we all just hung out and enjoyed each other's company. But the best thing about this arrangement was that, at the end of the day, he went home to his family and I went home to my son. No distractions, just my baby boy . . . and I loved it.

But now something was starting to change, there was a darkness that was slowly engulfing us. I couldn't put my finger on it, but something really horrible was beginning to happen. I could tell that JR was on pain killers constantly. I was starting to pull away and he felt it. I was ready to end our relationship, and I could tell it wasn't going to be pretty. JR wanted me to agree to marry him and then he would divorce his wife, but marriage was never the deal and not something I wanted. When I told him I wanted to end our relationship, he just laughed and thought I was joking. I made it clear I wasn't joking, but he wouldn't accept it. The catch was, he was my employer and had been for many years. How was I going to get another job? He started staying at my apartment overnight to make sure I wasn't seeing anyone else. Then he started staying and wouldn't leave. I finally called the police and they made me let him stay.

After spending years trying to build me up, he was now on a desperate mission to tear down everything he had helped create. He had become so jealous and obsessive that he never really allowed time for anyone else in my life. This was causing issues with my time for my son, and I needed JR out of my life. I just didn't know how I was going to get this done. I was pretty sure that he was hooked on pain killers now, and his entire personality had changed completely.

In the many years I dated this man, I had never seen him drink alcohol or take many pills at all. Now he was downing pain killers with liquor and mixing them with Xanax every day. I watched this amazing business man become a junky before my very eyes. He monitored everywhere I went and everyone I talked to. Because I had no family, I was an easy mark for him to control; there was no one else in my life but him and my little boy. I'll never forget the day our corporate attorney said, "Helen, you need to get a life." I wanted to say, "How can I? He won't let me have one, and he won't get out of my life so I *can* have one." I just shook my head and left. But this comment made me think, and it gave me the little spark of strength I desperately needed. Someone noticed something about my life and they cared enough about me to say something for my own good because they cared. Do you know how long I had waited for someone to notice me, not a man because I was a woman, but someone who cared about "ME," about my welfare. This man, out of the blue, made one simple comment that was meant to guide me in a positive direction, and no one had ever done that for me before. Having someone verbally confirm what I had been thinking all along was huge. This was a huge pivotal moment in my life. That one comment gave me the courage and the strength I needed to set out on a course that would almost consume everything I had inside me.

JR's sister suddenly got sick and was given 6 months to live. The week following her diagnosis, she was scheduled for surgery to remove a large tumor from her abdomen. When the doctors opened her up, they realized the cancer had spread all over her body and there was no way they could operate. While she was in the hospital, they decreased her time to 30 days at the most. As she lay in her hospital bed, I stroked her hair and she asked me to make a promise to her. She said, "You know, JR loves you very much. I need for you to promise me something. Will you promise me that you will take care of him?" I didn't want to promise her that; I knew I couldn't do it. I needed to get away from him, but I also didn't have the heart to deny a dying woman her last wish, either. I wanted her to be able to rest in peace, and I didn't have the heart to tell her that her brother had become an addict and a monster. So I said yes, merely to comfort her. She died shortly after that visit.

Every day I struggled with the promise I made to Dixie Lee and told God often that I knew I needed to get JR out of my life, but how could I break a promise I had made to a dying woman? I had always taught my children that you are only as good as your word. My foster mother had said that many times during our time together and it was engrained in who I had become. Mom often said, "Helen doesn't lie -- it's in the way she words what she says." So living up to something I said was very important to me. I think I was beginning to accept my fate because I knew I would *never* be able to break my word to her. I sealed my fate when I made her that promise. I felt like a caged animal trying desperately to escape but helpless to do anything about it. I feared for what was to become of my life and of my child's life. Had I sealed our fate the day I made that promise? How could I do such an injustice to my child? I felt like a terrible person and a horrible mother. Was my Uncle right? Was I truly unfit to be a parent? Look what I got myself and my child into. I asked God how was I going to make this right. How am I going to get out of this mess?

A few months later I decided to make a Christmas tree for Dixie Lee's grave. She loved birds and the nativity. I tried to decorate her tree with miniature ornaments that reflected who she was. I was sitting in the living room, the lights were dim and I concentrated as hard as I could on her and the essence of who she was. Christopher must have been out with some of his friends because I remember it being very quiet and me being the only one there. As I worked on her tree, I saw a glimpse of something moving down the hallway out of my peripheral vision. As I turned to look towards the hall, I saw a misty fog traveling down the hallway about 4 feet off the ground. As this misty fog traveled into the living room, I sat and watched with amazement and curiosity. At times, it was a little comical the way it moved and even rather cute. As it came into the living room, it slowed down almost to a stop as if to play with me. Then it sped back up and circled the Christmas tree very tightly. As it reached the top of this miniature Christmas tree, I felt Dixie Lee's presence. In my mind it was as if she were saying "Thank you for everything you've done for me" . . . or it was, "Thank you for loving me so much." (I was still too much in a state of confusion at that time to pick up on her exact message.) In my mind she said, "I never knew I was loved so much on this earth. It's okay, I know you can't keep the promise. To keep it would be detrimental to you." Then, in my mind, I saw the two of us playing as children around a beautiful tree in a pasture of tall grass. We were both wearing white dresses down to our knees and our long black wavy hair was blowing in the wind as we ran and frolicked as children do. Suddenly, for just a very quick moment, I saw me as that broken and battered little girl with a dead bird in my hands. Then, all of a sudden, all I saw and all I felt was this amazing warm brightness unlike anything I had ever seen or felt before. At that moment, I was suddenly cocooned in the most amazing brightness and love I have ever felt. I knew immediately in my heart that it was God's love. I saw this with my mind and with my heart. It was then I understood how God sees only what's in your heart because He connected directly with my heart and nothing else. He didn't care what I looked like or how I was dressed; all He cared about was my heart. For the first time in my life, for a moment in time, I knew what it felt like to have absolutely no burdens. God had lifted my burdens and all I felt was pure unconditional love. I remember looking up to heaven as I basked in this amazing love, and it was then I realized that He was showing me how much He loved me. Even as that little girl in the woods who was yelling and screaming at him, He didn't hate me, He loved me. I knew then that He was telling me in His own way how much He loved me when I was that broken little girl screaming at Him. As the brightness started to diminish, I begged Him not to go. It felt so good to finally feel unconditional love and I didn't want it to go away. I begged Him, but He said to my heart and mind, "It's not your time yet. There's something important you have to do first." I could tell that this "something important" was something huge, something wonderful, almost as if it could be something life changing. Then I saw a silhouette of a man in front of all this brightness. All I could tell was that he had kinky hair and bright light coming from his eyes. And the message I understood was "It will be in his eyes." And, just like that, everything was gone. I had often asked God, "How do you know a man loves you when you've never known love, except that of a child?" I knew then, that someday in my life, there would be a man with kinky hair who would love me very much and I would know that because it would be in his eyes. I didn't understand the kinky hair part, because all I thought about was a man of color and I didn't know anyone who fit that bill. But that wasn't the important thing,

I knew God loved me and that God truly does live. I knew at that moment that God loved me so much that He gave me the greatest gift of my life, The Gift of God's Love!

As I stood in confusion and euphoria, I suddenly heard a stuffed bear play a song from beginning to end. I had picked up a broken stuffed angel bear that reminded me of something Dixie Lee would like, and I purchased it in memory of her. It never played more than one note at a time and only if you hit it in the head for every note, but it reminded me of her. However, this bear was across the room and for the first time ever, it played the entire song from beginning to end without anyone touching it. As I listened, I felt this amazing euphoria. I remember wishing I could bottle this feeling for times when I needed something to keep me going. It seemed as if God was giving me confirmation that this did indeed happen and wasn't just a figment of my imagination. No matter what I did, this bear would never do that again.

Things with JR went from bad to worse, but I eventually managed to get him out of my life. That would be after he tried choking me to death, after he broke in and stole my car keys and everything I had locked up in the trunk for fear that he would break into my home, after he stole my car keys so I couldn't get to work and after he continued to wreck havoc in my life over and over and over again. I lost my job because he constantly called and the receptionist was fed up with it. Of course, they said it was due to a lack of work; but it was mainly because of him. Someone had broken into the building and had stolen information out of the owner's file cabinet. It was right before Thanksgiving, and I was having a hard time trying to find another job with it being the holiday season. Thank goodness I had some savings put away to keep me going for a little while. Once again, I found myself on my knees with my face in my hands begging God to help me put my life back together again. This time I promised I would never do THAT again!

On Christmas Eve I found myself sitting in the living room with a newspaper looking for any job that I could get. I found an interesting job for an insurance company; and I faxed my resume on Christmas

Eve, practically begging for this job as my Christmas present. The job was through a temporary agency; and in the next few days, I was called in for an interview. They sent me to the company and I sat down with a woman named Gail who was the head of Human Resources. I practically begged and promised I would make her very proud. I interviewed with the rest of the team I would be working with; and although I wasn't fully qualified for the job, she gave me a chance to prove myself. I told her that I was a quick study and wouldn't let her down. She also put the pieces together about what had happened and why I had no references except for our corporate attorney who said he would give me a recommendation. He obviously realized I was in a pickle. She recommended that I not to get "involved" with anyone there, especially since all the men were married. I immediately told her that would absolutely NOT be an issue.

I only had three days to learn my job from the woman who was leaving. She was trying to leverage the fact that it was report time, that she was the only one in that office who knew how to do this report and wanted to renegotiate her employment. I think she didn't think anyone could learn the job that quickly and was hoping I would not be able to do it and would have to call her back in. However, I truly was a quick study, very intuitive and knew I needed to learn all I could before she ever walked out the door. I made a promise to Gail, and I was determined to do everything I could to make her proud of me. I worked diligently on the statutory accounting report that I was supposed to work on and was able to have it completed accurately within the allotted time. With a lot of hard work, we reached our deadline and everyone celebrated with profit sharing checks. Although I had only been there for a few weeks and was not even their employee, they decided they would give me a check as well. They also rewarded me by buying out my contract and making me a full-time employee. This allowed me to be eligible for health benefits for both Christopher and I. This was the start of "me time." This was my time to concentrate on nothing but Helen and to start working on all of the broken pieces that needed repairing. In other words, I needed to rebuild Helen from top to bottom and everything in between.

One night out of the blue, the police showed up at my door with paperwork asking me to sign it. They informed me that they had arrested a man for stalking my apartment. Before the stalking was over, JR would be arrested more than once for stalking me. I never told the police anything; they came to me. They made it clear to him that, if they arrested him one more time, he would be doing time in prison. I had a guardian angel out there somewhere and I was so thankful.

Chapter 15

"Humpty Dumpty sat on a wall. Humpty Dumpty had a great fall. All the king's horses and all the king's men couldn't put Humpty Dumpty back together again."

How does one mend a broken heart and a broken life at the age of 35? How does a woman of 35 with the life skills of an adolescent figure out on her own how to think, react and reason like a 35 year old woman? With limited resources, time and energy, how does a person find the necessary strength to reach inside and do all that is required to change almost everything about themselves? With such a huge undertaking, how does one reach inside and find that kind of strength without anyone to guide, educate, or push the desire? How does one find the necessary desire to even broach an enormous undertaking such as this? I tell you, my friend, I didn't do it alone; my Father was there and He pushed me. He wanted what was best for me, and He guided me to the resources necessary for an undertaking such as this. My Father made it clear there was something important I had to do before my time was up on this earth, and He put me on the path to change. He guided me to the necessary tools to overcome the incredible ineptness in my life. It all started with a little book I accidently found about decision making.

I searched the internet for anything I could find about decision making, and I found a book written by a minister named Andy Stanley. The book was called, The Best Question Ever. It gave a formula for making good, sound decisions. Because I was a spreadsheet guru, I could relate to a formula. It was as if he wrote this book just for me. A formula . . . this was defiantly something I knew I could apply to my life. After reading this book, I decided that before I made a decision, I would put it through this test first: What is the wise thing for me to do, in light of my past experience, my present circumstances, and my future hopes and dreams?

First I had to allow myself to set a future goal, which was huge for me. I NEVER set future goals. Foster children don't often do that, and I never allowed myself to think in terms of "the future." After setting my future goal, every decision I made was to get to that goal. I typed this formula on paper and I hung it everywhere I could. It was on my mirror, on the lamp beside my bed, in my car, on my computer screen at work, and on my telephones. It was everywhere. I left them taped up for about a year. After about a year, this modified behavior then became habit. This book changed my life. This was another one of life's defining moments for me.

By now, the guy who was stalking me was still stalking me but not as badly as he had been. There was one day shortly thereafter that he stopped altogether. Years later I found out his son was in a really bad accident and they weren't sure if he was going to live. That distracted JR and I didn't see him again or hear from him for many years.

This allowed me to start putting my life and myself back together piece by piece. I think some people at work thought I was a little stuck up, but what they didn't realize was that I was a nervous wreck. I just needed to be left alone so I could concentrate on nothing else but my son and me. This time of change and repair required everything I had inside of me. Years passed and, as I opened up and started sharing little bits of my life, it became a much warmer environment. Eventually this group of coworkers would become my family. They were the only people in my life at that time, outside of my son and daughter. Tanya was calling me often, and she even came to stay with me before going into the Air Force. She had finally come to learn that a mother's love is unconditional and that I was there for her no matter what. She was no longer the party girl and was becoming quite a wonderful young lady. I didn't compromise my rules; and when she was ready, she came home. My foster parents had a saying, "I'm your parent, not your friend." I was realizing what a wonderful foundation I had and I owed it all to my foster parents and my family at Emmanuel Baptist Church of Kerkrade. Not everyone would agree with me, but I felt good enough about myself to not care what others thought but to stand firm on my beliefs and how I felt about myself....finally!

By this time I had found Mom again. She had remarried and was living in Pooler, Georgia. Mom and I were starting to have a better relationship, and I really liked her new husband. I was starting to love myself more and this was allowing me to care more for Mom, as well. I think Mom had also found closure to some personal issues in her life at that time. I think together we found our individual selves; and in that, we were *finally* able to find "our" relationship. We were starting to slowly carve out a unique bond between the two of us.

Taking this time to "find myself" was really good for me and for my relationship with my children. Christopher and I spent a lot of time together. One day while I visited Mom, she suggested I start dating again. I wasn't real excited about the idea, but she told me about eHarmony anyway. I just kind of shrugged it off. Then a few weeks later Gail at work had suggested the same thing. It had been several years and everyone thought I needed to put myself back out there, especially since Christopher was a senior and would be leaving for college soon. I wasn't real excited about the idea but felt for the first time in life that maybe I was truly ready to give myself to someone else. I had been a single mother for about 14 years by that time, and the prospect of a serious relationship that might lead to marriage was a little easier to stomach.

After much hesitation, I decided to sign up for eHarmony; however, it took a few weeks for me to *slowly* fill out my application. Although I was feeling a little bit like a loser signing up to date online, I quickly decided I really liked it after deleting handfuls of guys I didn't care for. After this I began to look at it as a very good screening tool, especially after my last scary relationship -- great guy turns into a complete and total lunatic. Arrogant guys – delete; guys mentioning "you know what" – delete; guys wanting obvious second incomes – delete. A few guys I would talk to online and decided, no – delete; a couple of guys I met one time for dinner in a very public location and thought, no – delete. And, then, there was one guy I had a couple of dinners with and decided to give him my telephone number.

Rick and I got along pretty well. He was a great talker and I was a great listener. With Rick I didn't have to say anything . . . he talked enough for both of us, which was okay with me. He was a lot of fun and we enjoyed some of the same activities, but I don't think I was moving fast enough for him. He was concerned that he didn't know anything about me. How do you go about sharing when you have a past like mine? Although JR and I had talked about anything and everything, it took years for us to get there. Rick was very outgoing, very vocal and sort of "in your face" in a nice sort of way, but loud nonetheless. I really liked spending time with him. He was a lot of fun, but I wasn't sure about getting serious with him. I was questioning whether or not I was a good fit for him. I was still finding it really hard to get close to any guy, and he was getting pretty frustrated with it. We spent every weekend together; but I still couldn't let myself trust him enough to share my thoughts and feelings with him, much less my past. I was still in a pretty fragile state of mind, and I don't think he realized that when he called me from out of town and started arguing with me. I could tell he wanted me to argue back, but I wouldn't and that made him even madder. As he was yelling at me, I started crying; and when he finally realized that, I think it made him feel bad. When he got back from his trip, I started thinking about ending our relationship. I didn't think I was ready for someone with such a strong personality but thought I would give it a little more time. He was a very driven and brilliant man. I needed for him to handle me with softer gloves, but I wasn't able to express this to him. If I could have conveyed this to him, I think eventually we could have had a phenomenal relationship; but it was going to take a lot of time and moving slowly through the process. I don't think Rick was open to moving slowly and gently; it seemed as if he was ready to check marriage off of his to-do list.

What he did do for me was to awaken me. Rick kept asking, "What would you like to do?" "Where would you like to eat?" "What do you like to do, Helen?" He would get rather frustrated when I continued to answer, "I don't care. Whatever you want is fine with me." It finally struck me that I truly didn't care, but I didn't care because I never really gave this much thought. My life was centered around keeping other people happy, and it never occurred to me to think about what I wanted. I had no idea what I wanted or what I liked. Rick awakened something in me, and I knew I had a lot more work to do before I finished putting me back together. I needed to find Helen.

During my relationship with Rick, I got a call from my sister, Vicky. She said that my dad was dying and they didn't expect him to live but a couple of more months. Dad called and talked with me. He kept telling me he loved me; and I said to him, "Dad if you truly love me, prove it. Tell Vicky you're sorry for what you did to her. She needs closure. She's having a hard time moving on, and she needs for you to set her free." He said he would, but I didn't hold out much hope for it.

Vicky called a few days later and said Dad asked me to come and visit, I asked her if Dad had apologized for what he did to her. She said that he hadn't; and I told her no, I wouldn't go visit. She was so mad that she slammed the telephone down on me. The next day she called again and said the same thing except that the doctors had changed their estimate to about a month. I still wouldn't go visit him. A few hours later she called again and said that they were only giving him a couple of weeks. I was starting to get a little annoyed about the phone calls because it was getting close to report time again at work, and I was the only person who knew how to do that particular report. I worked for an insurance company, and this was a required regulatory report with a deadline. The penalties for late or inaccurate reporting were very stiff. Again, I told her no. However, this time I talked to God about it. I told him that I've been making the decisions here and asked if I had the right to keep my father from seeing me before he died. I thought hard about it and realized that it wasn't my place to make this decision, but God's place. I already had one huge regret that I had to live with every day about Dottie's death, so I told God that I was putting this one in His hands. So I picked up the phone and called my sister and told her that I was packing and would be leaving the next day after I stopped by my office to let them know. Once I did that, I kid you not, two hours later my sister called to tell me Dad was gone. I truly feel that God handled it for me; and to this day, I have absolutely no regrets for my decision.

The next day I left to attend Dad's funeral. Christopher was away at college so I went by myself. He was attending a military college. It was his first year and things were a little rough for him, so I didn't even call to tell him. When I got to Columbia, South Carolina, I went over to the funeral home for my dad's viewing. My brother and sister met me there. When we went inside, we found that Dad's wife and our half-sister had put pictures of Dad with his "other" family on the inside top of the casket but none of him with his "original" family. My brother went nuts about this and started taking down the pictures. There was an argument; and he threatened to come back with a gun and blow everyone's head off, including the funeral director's. Once again, the family was pushing us out of the picture. They caused us to be without family our entire life and now there they were punishing us for not being a part of the family. I found this utterly disgusting, but I kept it to myself.

The next day we were all at an aunt's house discussing the funeral with the preacher. The "other" family was telling the preacher wonderful stories of a loving dad who cared for them and took care of them. Our side of the room was quiet. The only "wonderful" story we had to tell was the time Dad spanked me for my spelling words. We didn't have any good stories to tell. After hearing way too many wonderful things Dad had done for his "other" family, Danny had all he could take and had to get out of there. Dad put us through a life of constant trauma and horror, and we had to sit and listen to all of the wonderful things he did for his "other" family.

On the day of the funeral, as we formed the procession line, my aunts decided that a young boy my dad had become very fond of would be first in line and would lead us in. Danny was livid, and there was no calming him down. How dare they try to take away his honor of being the oldest and leader of our family? Granted he was a mess, but what could they expect after the kind of life he was forced to live? My life was bad, but the life he lived made mine look like a fairy tale. They had a hand in creating his issues and now they were shaming him. How dare they treat him like that! Once again, our family was putting some other kid who was merely an acquaintance above us. This family caused us to go through a horror-filled life our entire lives, and they still had absolutely no respect for us even then. How could they treat us like that? It was their fault that we weren't around them most of our lives, not ours. We were little children thrown to the wolves by our family. How dare they judge us and penalize us for it. Our entire lives we were penalized by our biological family because they decided to wipe their hands of us as babies. But this is the reality of life for foster children every day. The lives foster children live don't even begin to resemble lives ordinary children have. How can you punish a child for condemning them to a life they never asked for or deserved?

Danny made enough of a scene that they allowed him to be the first in line; but after we got inside, he sat against the wall and kept banging his head against it. By now I had an incredible headache that was quickly turning into a migraine. I reached over and calmed him down several times. While I was calming him, I heard the preacher say that Dad accepted God into his heart at the very end, and he seemed pleased Dad did so. I was shocked at my reaction.... I was angry. I was so angry that this man who had caused so much pain to so many people would be allowed to go to heaven. I couldn't understand it! How could God allow him to rest in eternity with us, with my mother and my sister? How dare He?! I feel better about it today, but sometimes I still struggle with this. I know it's not a Christian-like reaction; but in real life, I often find this very hard to accept. I'm also bewildered that I would allow myself to feel angry about something like this.

For some unknown reason, I agreed to sing "Amazing Grace" with my step-sister, who I didn't know from Adam, but agreed to it anyhow. As I stood up and stepped onto the stage where Dad's casket was and started to sing, I suddenly realized how badly my head ached and how nauseous I felt. As I sang, I kept stopping and starting, trying not to throw up on him. I quietly begged God not to let me throw up on him. I remember saying "Please don't let me throw up on him. Please, oh please, don't let me throw up on him, God." Somehow

I managed to finish the song and sit back down. At the end of the funeral, people kept going up to the podium to say wonderful things about this evil man. He was wonderful to everyone it seemed, except for his first family. After hearing sickening story after sickening story, I had to get up and set the record straight. I couldn't let this man be buried as if he were a hero. I was surprised that my brother and sister didn't stand up to say anything; I waited . . . but nothing. I was hoping they would, so I wouldn't have to, but still nothing. So I got up and said something like, "This man was a terrific man to a lot of *other* people; but this man was my father and he had no I idea I could even do that (referring to the singing)." I don't remember the rest because all I remember after that was begging God to not let me throw up on him. Somehow I managed to finish what I was saying and sat back down. Everything else is just a blur.

I rode to the cemetery in the family limousine with Dad's sisters; but my brother and sister wouldn't ride in the same car with them and were angry with me for doing so. I was trying to split my time between the families so no one would think that I liked the other better. In the limousine all I could do was lay my head back on the seat and close my eyes to keep the nausea at bay. That worked for a little while and I got through the burial; but after they put the casket in the ground, I ran and threw up at every tree between him and the car. My brother-in-law drove while I sat in the back seat throwing up in a bag that was stuffed in the back of the seat of the car. I was so sick and so incredibly embarrassed.

They took me back to my cousin's house, and I think I remember them feeding me some medicine and tucking me into bed. I do remember by cousin coming in and kissing me on the forehead. I thought that was so sweet. The next day I felt better and headed back home. I was mentally and physically exhausted but well enough to drive back home.

When I returned home, Rick made a comment that he thought I should have invited him to the funeral. I told him about it and that was the first real glimpse I gave him into my life. My dad's death was a very emotional time for me and it really took a toll. I felt very defeated, and I started writing my memoirs. I wanted to empty my mind of all the bad memories to make room for good memories. I think maybe I felt Dad was gone and so it was time to rid my brain of the stories and little details about our horrible life so I could start a new life with fresh memories. So I sat for hours, purging the old, to make room for the new. I don't think I was very good company during his time. My relationship with Rick didn't last very long after my dad's funeral. He wanted more from me than I could give at the time, and I wasn't sure I would ever be able to get more serious. So I thought it best to cut my ties and move on.

Later on, I got a call from my brother and he told me about Dad's will. Dad didn't have much and I wanted absolutely nothing from him. However, what he left for the three of us was rather shocking. Even in Dad's death, he was a mean and selfish man. He left the three of us letters. I never received mine, but my brother and sister read mine to me. It said something sort of like . . . he was always there for me when I needed him, and he had no idea what he did or why I had shunned him (using vulgar and ugly words that I can't repeat, of course). He couldn't understand why I kept his grandchildren from him. He spewed nothing but hateful words to the daughter who once adored him. He spewed hate at both of my siblings as well. This letter was all my father left me. In the end, he was still the same man he was the day I was born.

Chapter 16

The eHarmony candy store......Oh, how does one choose? This guy or that guy? They all sound alike. This one looks perfect and this one sounds nice. One or two? How many do I choose? Is this the one, is he Mr. Right?

Christopher was now finishing his senior year in high school and was preparing to decide which college he would be attending. Christopher was one of three Douglas County High School students nominated for prestigious positions at U.S. service academies.

The newspaper write up said, "Hilton, of Austell is on Gingrey's nominee list for the U.S. Military Academy (West Point), the U.S. Naval Academy, the U.S. Air Force Academy, the U.S. Merchant Marine Academy and Georgia Military College. Hilton has set his sights on piloting. In addition to working on the school newspaper, Hilton will earn CISCO certification for his expertise in computers.

U.S. Representative Gingrey had this to say, "These students and their parents have every right to be proud to be on this list. It's quite an honor." And proud I was!

I was so proud of Christopher, and I finally felt I had truly become a successful parent all on my own. Chris was extremely smart, very driven and very well behaved. I had done it. I had shown my family that I *am* a good mother. I finally convinced myself that, without their constant interference, I can truly be a great parent. I single handedly molded this wonderful, unique and special boy who was quickly becoming a man. I also realized that I would soon be completely by myself and that I needed to find a life of my own.

Eventually, I decided to renew my eHarmony account and continue building my dating skills. Although my heart still wasn't 100% in it and I wasn't sure if I would ever be able to get there, I knew I had to. I knew I had to keep pushing myself forward. I kept telling myself, "I can do this, I can do this."

It wasn't long before I met a guy named John. He seemed to be a very nice guy, and we decided to start talking to each other through the eHarmony network. After a few emails, I decided to give him my cell phone number, and we had a couple of telephone conversations before meeting in person. Then we decided to meet for dinner at Garrisons, a very public restaurant close to where I worked. During dinner, John asked me if I wanted to join him for a get together at his house that weekend. John had just bought a new house and was having a house warming get together for his friends. I accepted; and after the get together, he asked if I wanted to join him and his Tampa friends on a boating trip the following weekend at a lake in South Carolina. It wasn't an overnight trip, so I again accepted. I think John was rather surprised and pleased that I was adventurous enough to keep up with him and the guys while the other women remained in the boat during some of the more physically demanding activities. However, I did draw the line when they decided to dive off an incredibly high rock. John said he was pleasantly surprised at my ability and desire to be very feminine and classy, yet tom-boyish and rugged at the same time.

John traveled a lot for work, but we continued to see each other almost every weekend when he was in town. It wasn't love at first sight, but we were comfortable with each other. We were both very leery of new relationships, and I think it took time for both of us to trust each other. He didn't push for us to grow quickly and I was very comfortable with that. He didn't push for conversation, but let me quietly just be and I was happy with that. John was a very busy man; and if he wasn't out of town on business, he was typically on his cell phone talking business when he was home. So a quiet, comfortable relationship was a perfect fit for him. Due to his demanding job, I don't think John had had very many serious relationships even though he was in his early 40's. It seemed that dating wasn't very high on his priority list. I didn't know what his story was; he wasn't giving out a lot of personal details. That was okay with me because neither was I. I could tell there was something in his past keeping him from getting too close, and he made it clear that it would be a very long and patient journey to get into his heart-- not so much with words as with actions.

After a few dates, I was pretty sure John was still dipping into the eHarmony candy store and I let him know I wasn't happy about it. I explained to him that he would never be able to build a relationship with a woman if he didn't focus on one woman at a time. I also let him know that I was a one-man, one-woman kind of gal and that he had to commit to only me or move on. He said that made sense to him, and he decided to close his eHarmony account. I was pleased with his decision and we continued to see each other.

As time passed, our relationship slowly grew and we made sure we took our time getting to know each other. About three months into our relationship, John told me he wanted to do things differently this time, that he wanted to wait until he was married before being intimate. John was 42 and had never been married. He said that he felt that maybe adding intimacy to a relationship before marriage in the past had been the reason for it not progressing to the next level. He also said that he was ready to take a relationship to the next level but that he wanted to do it God's way this time around. My first reaction was, "You've got to be kidding me!" Then, "Humm…He must be seeing someone else besides me." Doing things God's way is not something you typically hear from men, so I was rather shocked. But, in time, I found he truly wanted to do things differently this time around.

So, I started traveling the 45 miles to visit him and started going to church with him. Believe it or not, his preacher was Andy Stanley, the author who wrote the book that changed my life. This gave me a sense of peace that I felt I was following God's plan for my life . . .

for a change. I had been going to church off and on throughout the years but never felt at home with any of the churches I attended. None of them had that homey, family feel that my church in Holland had had. Not even this one. It was a huge mega church. I enjoyed it, but I just couldn't feel that at-home feeling that I desperately longed for. Don't get me wrong, Andy was a phenomenal preacher. I loved hearing him teach, but I still felt lost.

About a year after we started dating, one day while at work, I looked over at a picture I had taken of John and a friend's little boy when I noticed his hair. He needed a haircut; but because it was a little longer than normal, I noticed the "kinky" hair like I had seen that day in the silhouette. I smiled because I knew once again that the misty fog I saw that day really happened and I knew this was the man God had created just for me. I knew then that one day I would marry the man in this picture, that one day he would be my husband.

It wasn't long after this revelation that I invited John to meet Mom and Dad Chase. During our visit, I left the pages of notes I had written for my hoped-for future memoir on the bed in his room. That night when he retired to his room, I assume he found the notes and started reading because, during the night, I heard him go to the bathroom and blow his nose. He never mentioned the notes or what he had read, but I know he read it and that it had an emotional effect on him. I couldn't bring myself to speak of the things that happened in my life, but I was able to put them on paper and give the man in my life something to read that would allow him to see a glimpse of the shattered woman he was dating. I was surprised that he didn't talk about it, yet relieved because I knew any response by me would be emotional. I felt relieved that I was able to enlighten my future husband before we pursued a more serious relationship. This was a first for me.

Our relationship was still moving rather slowly and I wondered many times if we would ever "get serious." After dating for about 8 or 9 months, I finally told John I loved him. John explained to me that he had heard that from women before only to have them end their relationship shortly thereafter. He also said that he had never told a woman that he loved her. I trusted what John said because John always chose his words *very* carefully. I could tell that he wanted to be absolutely sure that anything he said to me would in no way mislead me into thinking there was anything more between us than a mere dating relationship. I wondered many times if not allowing an intimate relationship between us was keeping him from letting me into his heart. John was even very careful about how we kissed to make sure we didn't cross any lines. I struggled many times with our decision but prayed about it and stayed the course. He wasn't allowing me close to him in any way, and I couldn't decide if he had issues or if he truly felt that it would cause us to give in to intimacy. I decided to move forward with caution and much patience.

On December 24, 2005, John told me he loved me for the very first time. We had been dating for 1½ years. I had secretly planned to end our relationship on December 31ˢᵗ if he had not told me he loved me by the end of the year. I had prayed many times before then about John's inability to love me and was wondering if I understood God's path for my life with John correctly. I tried to explain to God that, if He would just write down instructions, I would be more than happy to follow His every command; but He has yet to do this for me. Seriously, wouldn't this be so much easier? Then I would know every day whether I was truly following His path for my life or, once again, etching my own little path off His. I had become an expert at doing that. So, I was relieved to hear those words from John at last. I had begun to wonder if he was able to love a woman or if he was going to continue to guard his heart until the end of time.

In August of 2006, John and I attended a premarital weekend with Growing to Oneness Marriage Ministries. We spent the entire weekend learning about ourselves, each other and how compatible we would be in a marriage to each other. At the end of the seminar, we wrote letters to each other and created a Marriage Mission Statement together. We enjoyed the weekend and I think we felt closer to each other than we had our entire dating relationship. It made us discuss the hard stuff. John and I are both very passive and tend to just sweep things under the carpet instead of discussing them. So, this was good for us; it made us discuss them.

Finances and parenting were my two deal breakers. We discussed finances and it seemed that we were both on the same page with that one. We both agreed to live on a monthly cash basis and to carry no debt except for mortgage payments. I felt pretty confident that our actions and words matched and that we were in complete agreement on this issue. Our next issue was parenting. Because we knew more children were in our future, I needed to be sure we were on the same page with this one, as well. Although John didn't have children, he had seen my parenting techniques and didn't seem to have an issue with my parenting style. We agreed that we were both firm parents and were on the same page with parenting. These are two areas in life where I have very strong opinions and don't often compromise in either category. So, being certain we were on the same page before marriage was extremely important. If we weren't together on either issue, I would have ended our relationship immediately. I was very pleased and extremely relieved that we were together on both of these major issues.

Two weeks after our premarital seminar, John took me to lunch after church. We went to the Garrison's restaurant where we had our first date. After we parked, John took my hand and started talking to me about our dating relationship. If you know John, very seldom does he ever talk about anything deeper than surface level; so this was rather puzzling to me. Then he asked me if I would marry him. Believe it or not, I was so shocked that he finally got around to asking me, that I forgot to answer him. However, I'm pretty sure he knew the answer anyway. I had made it quite obvious that marriage was something I was ready for. I'm thinking the email with a picture of the ring I wanted, the name of the store, and how he could combine discounts to maximize his hard earned dollars was a sure indication that the answer would be "Yes!"

On December 9, 2006, after almost three years of dating, John and I were married in a cute little white church that was over 100 years old. I was thrilled to have my children in our wedding. My daughter was my maid of honor, and my son walked me down the aisle. My foster father danced with me for the father-daughter dance, and my foster mother was in the Bride's Room with me. My sister Vicky and my foster sister Sally were there, as well. That was the extent of my family. My biological family was invited, but none of them – with the exception of Vicky -- even bothered to respond.

I was very nervous before the wedding and started to second guess myself. Was this really what I wanted? I still had some unanswered questions, but was I being too careful? Was I ready to give up 17 years of single life? Is he truly the "right guy," or was I making another mistake? Just as I was starting to panic, they rang the bells, opened the door and I stood there looking at my husband-to-be. As I looked into his eyes, I felt a calmness sweep over me and I knew this was the man I was supposed to "do life" with. This was the man God had created just for me. My son took my arm and guided me to this man waiting to be my husband. His eyes were sparkling as he smiled an enormous smile; then he looked down at me and quietly said, "You're beautiful." At that moment, I thanked God for bringing this wonderful man into my life.

We had a beautiful wedding and I was glad we decided to "go all out." I wasn't sure how I was going to handle being the center of attention and was a little embarrassed that I didn't have much family or many friends to invite. But I enjoyed the day and was elated to share it with so many wonderful people. My children both love John and were ecstatic to see us both very happy. We danced the night away with friends and family until it was time to leave.

John and I decided to stay at a hotel close to the wedding reception rather than at home so his friends wouldn't crash the honeymoon night that we had waited three long years for. We also made sure we stayed at a different hotel than our guests and informed the people at the desk not to give out our room number under *any* circumstances. John and I ate breakfast with our guests the next morning and then flew to beautiful Hawaii for our honeymoon. Finally! I had found a little piece of heaven on earth.

Sally, Dad Chase, Mom Chase, Me, John, Tanya, Vicky, Christopher

Chapter 17

John and I talked about children before we were married. He had informed me that he desperately wanted children; and, since I was unable to have more children myself, he was fine with adoption. I told John that I didn't feel the need for more children but didn't feel I could deny the immense joy of children to someone I loved either. I knew that, while growing up, children were a must for me; and I couldn't imagine denying anyone something that important and wonderful. John and I were both 46 by this time and I didn't want to wait much longer. When we discussed children, I told John I only wanted to adopt from the foster care system. I know the pain and heartache hundreds of thousands of children suffer every day, and I wanted nothing more than to save one of them from the pain and horror of foster life. He agreed, and we started attending impact classes through the Fulton County Department of Family & Children Services. We had to drive to the other end of Atlanta once a week for 6 weeks, but we finally finished our classes. I was surprised and appalled to see the caliber of people applying to be foster parents. Several of them had just been in the United States for six months and could hardly speak English. Many of them seemed poverty level, a few of them were elderly, and a lot of them were single. It seemed as if only a slight few were really good candidates to be a right fit for the demanding task of raising a foster child. I heard later that many of them did become foster parents, but I'm not certain of the number.

We finished our impact classes and started on the home study process. When the home study process was completed, I learned that the bank I was working for had decided to move their regional offices further into Atlanta. The drive from Alpharetta where we lived to work was a lengthy drive; and, with a traveling husband and upcoming children responsibilities, I couldn't imagine driving further into Atlanta. So, I took a demotion and transferred to a branch in Alpharetta to allow me to work while parenting. I am very driven and have worked my entire life; I could not imagine myself not working. Then, believe it or not, right after I transferred to the branch, they changed their hours. John traveled a lot and the new hours weren't compatible with children and a traveling husband. So after a little while at the branch, I gave my notice and quit. This was a very hard decision for me because I really enjoyed working. It was part of the foundation of who I was, but I knew deep down that it was a sacrifice I needed to make for the sake of my family. I really hated to let this job go. You see, I had not been looking for a job change when, out of the blue, the bank called me and asked me to assist their regional president. At that time I was working for the insurance company and they had become my family. But I felt a little stifled there because I had learned all there was to my job, and it had become pretty repetitive for me. Being challenged once again was something I craved. So, when the bank called me, I felt I had finally reached career success. I felt I had made it to the top. But regardless of the empowerment this position gave me, I felt I was needed elsewhere. I felt I had reached the first large goal I ever allowed myself to set; now it was time to start reaching God's goal. For many years I had believed that God had a higher purpose for my life, but I didn't know what that was. I felt he wanted me to write that book I had always talked about, but I kept telling him I had to work and it didn't allow enough time to write a book. Now I had no excuse -- I no longer had to work. So I told Him that in a couple of months I would start on the book I promised Him years ago.

A couple of weeks after I quit my job with the bank, I went to San Francisco with John. John works for a company that provides labor to install tradeshows and conventions nationally, so he travels a lot. When we got back from San Francisco on August 19, 2008, we had a meeting with our caseworker. I only wanted to foster a child that fit our criteria for adoption because I knew a lot of these placements turn into adoption. I also knew that, if you wanted young children, you typically needed to foster in order to adopt the little ones. I was teaching adoption classes in my spare time to help facilitate foster adoption, so I was pretty well versed on this subject. I only wanted one little girl, an infant to about 4 years old. That was all I wanted and I was pretty adamant about it. Our caseworker told us it would be a long time before we found the child I was looking for. John was pretty open to any child, although leery of diapers. I could tell John was ready to be a daddy and was willing to take almost any child he could. It was exciting to think I could help fulfill my husband dreams. I was totally and completely committed to giving this 150%. I couldn't wait to see my wonderful husband's eyes when a child called him "Daddy" for the very first time in his life.

On Thursday, August 21, 2008, I sat down to my computer. There was an email from our caseworker, which I opened and read. It was a flyer, an urgent request from DFCS. They were in desperate need of a foster-to-adopt family for a sibling group of three. If they couldn't find a family willing to take all three within a week or two, they would have to split them up. They were currently in separate foster homes, and they desperately wanted to bring them back together for adoption.

Here is what the flyer said:

> DFCS is searching for a foster-to-adopt home for a sibling group of three. Ellen is 5, Andrew is 2 (he will be 3 in December) and Billy just turned 2. These children are Hispanic with Caucasian ancestry. They have successfully been in the same foster home with each other for over 18 months. Ellen speaks fluent English, but can also understand Spanish and knows a few words of Spanish.

> Ellen is a beautiful little girl who is in Kindergarten and loves all things feminine—earrings, dressing up and the color pink! She has very long straight dark hair. She is a loving little girl who loves to please others. At times, she gets disappointed with her family life and has been known to throw temper tantrums. She is in therapy to address her feelings of loss regarding her family.

Andrew is a very handsome little boy who was born prematurely. He has straight black hair. He has come a long way since his birth and is on target developmentally. He has some digestive issues that are being treated by diet. Andrew is very loving and likes to be held when he feels uncomfortable in non-familiar situations.

Billy is also a very handsome little boy with curly brown hair. He, too, was born prematurely and has come to develop on track. He has some digestive issues that are monitored, also. He is very verbal and active!

Unfortunately, the foster home where these children resided has closed and we are actively seeking a permanent home for these children ASAP. The Termination of Parental Rights hearing is scheduled for Oct. 6, 2008. The children are presently in separate foster homes and need to be together. The home who has the boys has given us only one more week to move the children.

The mother is incarcerated and the putative fathers have not been active in their case. Prior to her incarceration, the mother did not visit with the children, nor did she work her reunification case plan.

DFCS is making a separate permanency plan for a younger sibling.

It was far from what I was looking for, but I thought I felt God tug at my heart. So I sent the flyer to John at work.

After a lot of discussion, we decided that we had a beautiful home with plenty of empty bedrooms and, if it was something God brought to us, we would be more than happy to share our blessings with children in need. John and I prayed, and then we put our name in the hat and left the rest up to God. On August 25th, I received a phone call from our caseworker saying they had selected another couple. She apologized and we told her it was okay. We told her we really didn't know what to do since we weren't sure if it was more than we could handle but that we had decided to let God make the decision and we'd be happy with whatever He decided. I was somewhat relieved but, surprisingly, a little sad. We didn't see any pictures; but they sounded like sweet children . . . a little challenging maybe, but sweet. Since I had raised children on my own and John and I seemed to be on the same page with parenting, I felt we would be okay with "a little challenging." So that didn't scare me too much.

On Tuesday, August 26th, at 7:30 a.m., I received a call from our caseworker saying that things had fallen through with the other family and that we were the only other couple on the list. The other family spoke Spanish but no English. My mind was racing as to how this couple was able to become foster parents to begin with. I was shocked at this piece of information; but knowing we had let God decide this, we immediately knew what had to be done. On Wednesday, August 27th, we drove about an hour away to meet with a team of DFCS workers and worked out the adoption specifics, what we were willing to accept and not willing to accept. We dug through medical histories, family histories and each child's personal needs. We never saw a picture of the children, just write ups, psychological evaluations, parents' backgrounds, etc. We walked outside with our caseworker who said, "You must have a direct link to God! I've never seen this happen *ever* in my entire career," and she was a very seasoned caseworker with over 20 years of experience. We told her that we had decided to put this in God's hands, and it was pretty evident what He wanted to happen here. We went in and told the group we were willing to take all three and asked them to say a lot of prayers for us. After we left, I was so stressed out and nervous that I threw up all the way home. It was a rather long ride home . . . poor John!

Although I had painted and decorated the nursery, we hadn't had time to furnish it yet. So that afternoon, our friends started bringing over everything anyone could ever need for small children. Within three or four hours, our nursery was ready to receive our two wonderful little boys. We sat that night and wondered what these two little strangers were going to be like. It was mind boggling to think that, in less than 12 hours, our big empty home would be full of little pattering feet. I couldn't believe that we had just been certified as foster parents for 8 days, and now here we were foster parents on the fast track to adoption, to boot!

I wondered if I was going to be able to love these two little creatures as much as I loved my own. I laughed at the thought of my husband's staunchly structured lifestyle and the havoc that reality was about to create in his carefully orchestrated world. Although I had no doubt he would love every minute of it, I also knew that he was about to have a huge reality check. I was very curious as to how this was all going to play out. I always love it when theory faces reality. This is when we learn the most about ourselves, our world and each other.

On Friday, August 29th, at 11:30 a.m. we opened the door to the two most adorable little toddler boys you could imagine. They immediately ran into our home and started looking around. We chatted with the children's caseworker for about 30 minutes on specifics for each child and then loaded several black garbage bags containing their belongings into the garage. When their caseworker walked upstairs to see their bedroom, she stepped in, hugged me and started crying. She said, "Oh, my gosh! Thank you!" She asked if we had decorated their room ourselves and we said, "Yes." She knew then that the boys where finally where they needed to be, that they would have a wonderful life and parents who would love them.

Our babies were 2 years old and we were already their 7th placement. Two years in the system, and they had already had seven different mommies and daddies! They had been ripped out of known environments and placed into the "world of the unknown" seven different times. What could be so bad that mere babies would face that ugly black hole that many times in two short years? I was completely blown away to know they had faced the beast seven different times. My, how brave they were . . . or were they? I was in awe, yet also very afraid. What happens to babies when they face the beast that many times in such a short period of time?

After the children's caseworker left, we literally looked at each other and said, "Okay, now what do we do?" We laughed at each other, then fed them lunch, showed them their room, played a little bit and put them down for a nap. They went to sleep right away as if new mommies and daddies were just a part of everyday life to them. Once I looked at those adorable little faces lying in their beds, I knew it was going to be okay, that God would give me the strength to persevere. These were my boys, my babies. They were finally safe and they were home. I knew at that moment that I would not have a problem loving these boys as my own. I think I must have fallen in love the moment their curious little faces ran into our home.

Billy was the baby; and when we put him down for a nap, we realized we needed to trade his bed for a crib. Billy had beautiful curly brown hair and beautiful big brown eyes that took in everything he saw. He was very alert and friendly to both of us the moment he walked into our home. He was happy and laughed about anything and everything. He was barely walking when he came into our home. Although he was technically 2 years old and had been for several days, he was really only about 1½ due to his premature birth. Billy fell a lot and it was obvious his muscle tone was still very weak. Billy was nonverbal and grunted for what he wanted. He was a good natured little boy almost all of the time. He weighed 22 lbs. when he came to live with us and wore Size 18-month clothes. Billy suffered from gastrointestinal issues and had toddler diarrhea. I noticed he was shaky when he woke up. There wasn't any note on this, so I don't think anyone ever picked up on it until then. Although Billy looked healthy, we would come to find that he was still somewhat medically fragile. We read a comment where he was labeled as a little lazy, but I believe this had to do with his significant lack of muscle tone and his shakiness. There was something going on inside this little body that had yet to be diagnosed. His other six mommies never picked up on these issues and I wonder why.

Andrew was almost 3 years old when he walked into our home. He was tiny for his age, extremely unhealthy and still in diapers. Andrew didn't make eye contact with me, but he did with John. He ran in with Billy but became a little frightened when I approached him. He was able to open up to John right away but not with me. I didn't push. Andrew weighed 24 lbs. and also wore Size 18-month clothes. His skin color was ashen and there was a lot of bruising on his little body. Andrew's eyes were almost lifeless. There was no sparkle in them and many times I wondered if his mind was somewhere else. He often had a blank look on his face and seemed very depressed. He was extremely moody and had constant tantrums, almost as if maybe he was autistic or something of that nature. Andrew made it clear that he didn't like me and wanted nothing to do with me. He would hit at me anytime I came close to him, especially if he was in John's arms. He attached to John immediately and spent a lot of time in John's arms. He was extremely needy and very clingy. Andrew, too, had toddler diarrhea but at a much more extreme level and was diagnosed with "failure to thrive." He was all boy and, even though he was unhealthy, was very strong for his age. Andrew loved to play and he put everything he had into everything he did. Everything Andrew did was done to the extreme. Everything was hyper -- hyper focused on TV, hyper play, hyper depressed, hyper loving or hyper shut down. So if Andrew was not being stimulated in some way, he would instantly zone out within seconds of non-stimulation. Andrew, too, was nonverbal and grunted for what he wanted. It seemed as if Andrew was developmentally delayed. I knew we had a significant issue with Andrew, but that wasn't a deal breaker for me. This beautiful loving, confused little boy needed a mommy and a daddy to help him overcome the many obstacles in his young little life; and I was *committed* to making sure this little boy had the opportunity to be all that he could possibly be. He needed me and I was committed to him no matter what. It would seem that six other mommies didn't care enough to see his obvious significant issues. I say "didn't care" because he had been in my house for less than 6 hours and it was obvious we had significant issues to address. Was he difficult to parent? Absolutely. However, this tiny little toddler desperately needed an advocate. I was his forever mommy and I was stepping up to the plate. He was a baby and he deserved so much more than he had been getting. As I watched his battered little body sleep, I vowed to see to it that no one would ever hurt or neglect this child again in any way and that he would get everything he needed to survive and become the best that he could possibly become in life!

Both boys were taken from their mother at birth and placed in foster care the day they left the hospital. It appeared as if there had been abuse/neglect during their foster care tenure. In other words,

America, **we** are to blame for the state of bad health these two boys were in when they walked into our home. Granted, they were born with some medical issues; but we had the obligation to help overcome these issues, not add significantly to them. These boys were babies and they were in such bad condition. I felt so sorry for them, but knew I had to keep that at bay. I know the worst thing to do for a foster child is to feel sorry for them and let that dictate the way I parent. I knew from my past, that I had to look beyond the abuse and help them forge a new path to a better tomorrow. I knew that at least now they were safe and were in a soft place to heal. I also knew I had to start teaching and remolding right away. By ignoring their many problems, precious years had already been wasted. I knew every day was valuable time for us to rewire any damage in their brains due to the drugs and alcohol in utero that we knew they had been exposed to, for us to make up for the parent/child interactions they had obviously missed in foster care, and to teach them everything they had not been taught that children their ages should already have been taught or exposed to. I knew from that first day that we had *a lot* to overcome with these two precious little boys.

When the boys woke from their naps, it was close to dinner time. As I started cooking dinner, the boys started screaming and crying -- not being "a little fussy," mind you, but all-out screaming and crying. Because I had worked all of my life and worked a lot, I was domestically challenged in the kitchen. I knew how to cook, but I was all thumbs and not quick when it came to cooking. I also had to concentrate really hard on what I was doing; so with the screaming and crying, I was a nervous wreck by the time I got dinner to the table. The boys ate as if they had never eaten before. They ate more than I did, and we actually had to make them stop eating. They cried when we took the food away, but we were afraid they were going to make themselves sick.

John had to bathe the boys because Andrew had a full-blown tantrum every time I got near him. He still wanted nothing to do with me. I remember telling God that I was so not expecting this. I knew at that moment that there was no way I would have been able to juggle what lay ahead for me while working a demanding job. God knew what He was doing when my job came to an end. He knew these children were going to need all of me. I knew that, too. I have to admit, I questioned the commitment we had made at the end of day one; but it only lasted for a few minutes. It was a lot to commit to, but something in me shook it off as I talked to my Father. Then I took a deep breath and flipped a switch that put me into motherhood overdrive. I knew I was going to need it for some time to come. I had to persevere for the sake of these poor little boys. I kept saying, "We can do it. We can do it. We *can* do it."

At the end of day one, I sat in my rocking chair rocking this little boy who was touching my face and calling me "Mommy." He kept touching my face and repeating "Mommy" as if trying to etch the memory of my face into his mind so he could remember who his mommy was when he woke. As I watched his little eyes close and his little mouth suck on a pacifier, I knew I had to do it. Mothers don't give up on their babies, and I was his mommy. I kept telling myself, "I can do this. I can do this. I *can* do this." I knew I couldn't turn my back on this sweet little boy who desperately wanted and needed a forever mommy.

I could tell we were going to have our hands full and we had yet to add Ellen to the mix. I was concerned . . . very, very concerned.

The following week, we took the boys to meet their sister, Ellen. As we sat at a table inside of McDonald's waiting, in walked the most adorable, beautiful tiny little ballerina ever. She was truly breathtakingly beautiful. She had just finished ballet class and was still in her little pink tutu. I watched as John's eyes filled with tears and his heart melted; I could tell he fell in love right then and there. She had instantly stolen his heart and she wasn't even ours. Then, the cutest little, prissy, sassy, arrogant, all-consuming little girl I had ever met came over to us. It was then I realized...she was mine! I said a quick prayer and bit my tongue many times. I watched as this beautiful little girl controlled her foster mother in a strategically choreographed ballet aimed to satisfy the little girl's most every whim.

After she left with her then foster mother and we were on our way back home, I said, "God, come here. We need to have a talk." I knew what He wanted me to do and I knew it wasn't going to be easy. I was terrified. However, I often hear all things are possible with God; and I was hoping that with Him and with a different set of firm rules and expectations, we would quickly modify some of her very demanding behaviors. I must admit, I was very scared about the whole situation after this meeting. I felt we had made a very big mistake by not having an in-home visit before accepting all three children. But I couldn't help going back to my life and the damage it did to our sibling group when we were split up. I wanted so badly to give the gift of sibling love to this little family, but now I was scared that I had just bitten off more than I could chew.

The write up on the children was obviously written by someone who knew this family from the outside looking in. However, if it had reflected the true situation, I never would have considered all three. But the deal had already been sealed and God needed us for this little family. Was it going to be hard? Absolutely. But I kept telling myself, "With God anything is possible. We can do this. We can do this. *We* can do this."

"Faith, is not knowing God can; it's knowing that He will."[2]

---

[2]   Author Unknown

Chapter 18

My two little boys and their precious little sister were in such bad shape. How did this happen? How can the needs of babies go unmet? I am saddened and I am angry. How can we just turn our heads and allow our children to suffer like this? My Father . . . He must be so hurt by our utter disrespect for His commands to care for His children. But I will step up to the plate and do what six other mothers didn't do before me. I will care for His children, for *these* children and bring them back to health. Then I will bring them to Him, back to His house. He will guide me and I will follow Him. Together we *can* do this......or can we?

On Friday, September 5, 2008 we put the two boys into their car seats, added a third and drove to north Georgia to pick up our adorable little handful. Ellen had a school event, and we all met there to pick her up and bring her to her new home and family. The goodbye was tearful and our hearts went out to both Ellen and the foster mother. Her foster mother had wanted to adopt Ellen, but that would have meant splitting up the family. Again, had I known the true state of this little family, we would have agreed to split them up immediately. I seriously thought about calling the children's caseworker to change our decision to adopt all three, but John was already in love with this little girl. How could I break my husband's heart without even giving it a try? I also desperately wanted them to have their sibling group intact so they wouldn't bear the hardships that I had to bear losing the only sense of family I knew. They deserved to stay a family, but I was very concerned with this decision.

On our one hour trip home, Ellen must have asked fifty times or more how far we still had to go. As Ellen sat in the back seat counting her dollar bills with nonstop chatter, she said, "Momma gives me a dollar every night to stay in bed. Whatchu gonna give me?" I asked her if she liked cartoons and she said, "Well . . . YES!" with a tone that implied, "Why would you even ask me such a silly question?" I said, "Cuz . . . if you want to watch cartoons, you have to stay in bed. If you don't stay in bed, you won't be watching cartoons." God and I had words again, as this tiny little person sat in the back seat smacking on candy and taunting her two little brothers with the candy she had in her purse but was unwilling to share.

The next phase of our lives was a very difficult phase, probably one of the most difficult of my life. Our lives took a turn unlike anything I could have imagined. This phase became so difficult, so unbelievable that I had a hard time believing once again that this was truly "my life."

The next day, the kids got up and watched cartoons and fought. I don't remember much as my world was foggy and rather upside down. Ellen spent her entire day trying to mother the boys and control their every thought and action. It seemed as if she wanted all the attention for herself and would do anything to get it. Constant conversation was one way she kept constant attention on herself. If she had you talking strictly to her, then you wouldn't be able to talk with either of her brothers. Andrew wanted all of the attention as well and would fall on the floor and have a tantrum every time things didn't go his way or he felt he needed a little hug, which was constantly. Billy just went with the flow but cried when someone took a toy from him, hit him, or knocked him down, which happened quite often.

Both of the boys continued to cry and scream every time they saw food. Every time I started cooking, they would scream and cry the entire time until I got the food on the table and into their hands. If you gave them a small snack to eat until the food was ready, they would gobble it up in seconds and then scream because there wasn't any more. Ellen didn't want me to cook. She wanted me to concentrate all of my time on her and then magically put food on the table. When she was ready to eat, she would get to her seat, bang her utensils on the table and say, "Where's my food?!" God and I had words again. In foster care, they must have had limited availability to food because all three would gorge themselves. They had no self-control and I had to stop them from eating before they made themselves sick. Sometimes they would put so much in their mouths that it would make them throw up. Even then, they would sometimes cry because you took the food away. It broke my heart to see children instantly turn into animals over food. I tried not to take it all personally; but when you are exhausted, sometimes that's not quite so easy. And since I was up with the baby over breathing issues several nights a week, exhaustion was rampant.

After a long, hard day filled with chaos, I would get into a hot tub and cry. I would think of my job that I desperately missed and my friends. Most of my friends were women I worked with and, as most working mothers know, you don't often have time for friends outside of work. In addition, I had moved 50 miles away to live where John lives, so I had left any friends who were nearby.

John was faced with traveling for the first time since the children came to live with us. By now, they had been ours for about three or four weeks. I wasn't looking forward to this at all. I knew things were going to be tough, but I had no idea they were going to be as bad as they were. John, too, hated to leave at such a stressful time; but work needed to be done, especially since I had given up my job to be a stay-at-home mom. That evening, after Ellen had gotten home from school, after dinner was eaten and the dishes done, I took the boys to my bathroom and gave them a bath. Of course, we went through the typical crying/screaming routine while I cooked. Needing to be sure she had my constant attention, Ellen stayed in the bathroom talking to me while I tried to bathe the boys. Andrew disliked me and wouldn't let me touch him or do anything for him, so bathing him was an all-out battle. He screamed the entire time I tried to bathe him and fought with everything he had in him when I tried to wash his hair. It seemed almost as if something had happened to cause Andrew to be terrified of women. I felt so bad for him, but I was doing the best I could.

When the boys were finished with their bath, I put fresh water in the tub and put Ellen in while I took the boys upstairs to get them ready for bed. Ellen was 6 now, and I felt she was old enough to be alone in the bathroom. During the entire 20 minutes it took to dress, read to and pray with the boys, Ellen sat in the tub screaming and crying as loud as she possibly could because she wasn't getting my attention. I faintly heard, yet chose to ignore her, at which time I thanked God for my bedroom being far away and her neck not being anywhere within my reach!! When I got back down to her, she said, "I was crying and screaming for you!" I said in a very calm voice, "Yes, Sweetie…. I heard you, and you are NEVER to act like that again. Do you understand me?" The evening progressed and the next day came. The needs were greater than one person could fulfill. After a second day of constant screaming from Andrew because John was gone, Ellen pushing Andrew down the stairs because she wasn't getting my constant attention, a sick baby who couldn't breathe, no sleep, constant screaming while I cooked, I had all I could take and I called John. I asked him if he could come home early. He said, "Sure." He was supposed to be gone for eight days and was thinking I meant in a day or two; but when I started crying uncontrollably, he decided to take the next flight home.

The first two months were very hard and I shed many, many tears. God and I argued many times, and I was ready to give up almost every day. Before the children came into our home, I sat John down and explained that his first instinct was going to be to fill that deep, dark pit in their heart with lots and lots of love and attention. I told him, however, that that is the worst thing you can do. If you do that, they will relate love to physical affection and constant attention; and the more you give, the more they are going to require until they suck the life out of you. I told him the best way to love these children is with firm, consistent, loving discipline. I told him these things not as a know-it-all, but as a foster child who has watched this unique phenomenon occur time and time again. But being a first time parent to three older children in a state of crisis was more than his heart could resist and their needs took over his heart -- which is actually admirable, but not practical in this situation. They demanded every minute of his day and every ounce of energy he had, so there was nothing left at the end of the day to give to anyone else. Since we didn't agree on parenting techniques and I was the firmer parent... the children wanted little, if anything to do with me.

Although I didn't like the way the children were being allowed to "own" our house, being a new wife, I thought I would give John enough time to take the reins and reel them in. I was trying to respect his position as leader of our family. After 2 ½ months of total chaos and being closed off in my room crying, I decided something had to change. I either had to leave or make changes in my home, so I brought everyone together and laid down some rules. There would be no more cartwheels, flips, or tumbling in the house -- walking feet only; and there would be no more physical contact play, yelling or screaming-- inside voices only. Every time Andrew had a tantrum, which was all day long, he would immediately go into time out. Ellen was no longer to have unsupervised time with either of the boys. She controlled everything Andrew did and was physically abusive to him. We no longer had free play as it was obvious the children did not know how to participate in constructive play. They didn't play. It was mostly fighting, hitting, arguing and throwing toys at each other -- complete chaos. Neither Ellen, nor Andrew had any self-control or boundaries, and both were extremely impulsive. There was something terribly wrong; and even though I kept telling DFCS and my husband, no one wanted to hear me. I talked with our caseworker and she helped me understand Reactive Attachment Disorder (RAD). I started reading everything I could on this disorder; and the more I read, the more it sounded like Ellen. Andrew would have to wait; I needed to find out what was going on with Ellen ASAP.

I tried to tell my husband that foster children fare much better with lots of structure, firm consistent discipline and a calm environment. I tried to explain to him that Foster children are master manipulators, not because they are bad children, but because their lives have merely been about survival and that it was very important they have clear, consistent boundaries at all times. However, it seemed as if John and his siblings thought I was damaged due to my past and was now abusing my foster children because of it. They did not understand how extremely important it was to set the tone of our home the moment the children entered our environment and keep that tone throughout without any disruption. This consistent, firm, loving, structured, disciplined, and *predictable* environment is what the foster child needs in order to learn to trust again! It might not seem like it, but the foster child typically, (unknowingly) craves for and thrives best in this type of environment. Will they adhere to it immediately on their own? Absolutely not! They don't know how to, and they are too scared to. But if you maintain that extreme consistent tone and expectations are noted upfront, they will eventually become the child they were meant to be ....in *their* timing, not yours. However, the more consistent you are, the quicker they adjust.

You *cannot* parent foster children as you would biological children. I was open to John and I educating ourselves together, which meant we would read and make sure we understood the material the same way and then prepare a parenting plan together. John had never been around the "foster way of life" and knew nothing about it. He was not open to educating himself further on it nor was he open to trusting information about it from me. So anything that strayed from the techniques of raising "ordinary" children, as he had become accustomed to, was unacceptable and he wanted nothing to do with it. John would not believe or hear that his children were, indeed, "different" and required a different type of parenting. To parent them as ordinary children would have been merely another form of neglect.

I created a very structured environment, which I learned was so important for foster children because of their chaotic background. I turned a chaotic environment into a structured, controlled, calm and academic environment. Our new structured environment was met with defiance every day. However, this was the only environment in which our children were slowly beginning to modify their behaviors. Ellen was way behind in school when she came to us. She was finally starting to learn, and I truly believe this controlled environment helped facilitate that. Even though the results were slowly becoming visible, John hated to be the bad cop and was angry with me for insisting that rules be followed. But everything I was reading said a controlled, structured environment was very important to foster children.

Billy was in the doctor's office almost weekly and at the emergency room often. He was up most nights for months at a time unable to breathe, so sleep was something I got very little of. I was exhausted and I got no support from anyone. We began to live in a divided house where there were two sets of rules, and I was a monster that no one wanted to be around.

I started reading more about Reactive Attachment Disorder and decided to follow some of the techniques Daniel Hughes talks about in his books. Ellen tried to control everything in our lives. I implemented words and actions that told her that I was the mother and in control and that she was the child. Once again, this was met with anger from my spouse and his family. They couldn't understand that I could never let my daughter feel that she was in control of me, our house, or our family. They thought I was being petty; I felt I was trying to modify overly controlling behavior. They didn't care to understand that the first time I allowed her to have control I would have to start from square one all over again. You can't just defer to a child with RAD. Because Ellen hadn't been diagnosed with RAD, in their minds it didn't exist; and she was a normal little girl who liked things her way. But I knew that Ellen's quality of life depended on her modifying these behaviors, and I had to stand my ground so she would have the necessary tools to streamline into "normal life" once she was out of survival mode.

Ellen was way behind in school so I worked one-on-one with her 2½ hours a day to bring her up to par academically. A ten minute homework assignment would take her hours to do. We struggled and struggled and struggled. Every new lesson was met with defiance. I had to push her and cheer her on. Then she would learn to do it and would be so excited. This cycle played out over and over. Ellen would be so proud of her new achievements. You could tell it would build her self-esteem, yet she constantly doubted herself. This was a continuing cycle for months. I think Ellen was so afraid of failing that she couldn't allow herself to try anything new. John couldn't understand that deep, deep down inside Ellen really liked me pushing her. Deep, deep down inside I could see and feel this little bit of excitement and then it would quickly be replaced by fear. I knew this because I had lived it. Did it make me unhealthy and unable to parent her; or did it help me understand where she was coming from and that, although she seemed angry at me for pushing her, she actually felt loved when I did? She knew I believed in her because I didn't lower my expectations of her. I knew what she was capable of, and I didn't back down when it pushed her out of her comfort zone. Some people tend to lower their expectations of foster children, which actually lowers their opinion of themselves. No, I am not a psychologist; but I lived the foster life and I know how some of the children feel. However, because of my belief in her, this amazing little girl went from learning her alphabet to reading on her own in 6 months. What an achievement! If I hadn't pushed her, Ellen probably would have been held back in kindergarten. The school said, "At least she is very tiny for her age . . .So, if she has to repeat kindergarten, it won't be so hard on her." No one wanted me to push her. I would hear, "Oh, she's had a hard time of it, so why push her?" and, "She has so much to overcome without worrying about how she does in school." To me, that is abuse! I knew she could do it. She just needed one person to believe in her and push her to do her best. Using her past to take the easy way out was not an option. She had gotten used to using that as power. I was determined to replace that power with a much bigger and better power: confidence and self-esteem. And she was building just that...confidence and self-esteem. I could see her smiling bigger and bigger. Believe it or not, she began to love our academic time together; and she began asking to learn new things. She started relating our education time to love and affection and she soon couldn't get enough of it.

Billy and Andrew went to daycare during the day; but since Billy was often sick, he spent a lot of time at home. This time had become Ellen's and my time; so, on the days Billy was home sick, Ellen would become jealous. Every time I had to leave the room, Billy would get hurt. He would "accidently" fall and have a huge egg on his head, or he would accidently run into her swinging arms and would "accidently" get slapped leaving a big welt across his face. So I had to start either taking him with me when I had domestic tasks to complete or gating her in her room until I finished my task. While I cooked, I tried to let all three of them watch cartoons; but there was one small wall between the kitchen and family room where the refrigerator was. I couldn't even cook without her coaxing the boys behind the wall and hitting them and hurting them. So life wasn't pretty and I was having a hard time keeping the boys safe. I talked with DFCS about this and couldn't get anywhere. They told me that they absolutely would not split the kids up. I wanted them to separate them until we got the boys under control, and then maybe add Ellen back in at a later date. They said no.

I had no choice but to neglect babies who were already in a state of crisis, because parenting all three in the manner they needed to be parented was too much for one family. I felt horrible about myself every day, I was neglecting innocent babies -- every day I had no choice but to be an abusive parent. I now understood why we were their 7th placement. This is very sad, but it is not always in the best interest of the children to keep the sibling group "the priority." Sometimes, keeping them together actually sets them up for failure and, in turn, causes even more trauma to children already in a state of crisis. One child with RAD in a sibling group can possibly mean the entire sibling group will become unadoptable or, worse yet, have to constantly move from one home to another, as in this case. One move, one living disruption, is so traumatic, so devastating that any one move can be that "one move" that could cause a child to become traumatized to the point of no return. It's almost as if every move potentially carries the same trauma of a person being sentenced to death row. "The unknown" is truly *that* horrible, *that* devastating.

I jumped and screamed at DFCS so loudly that they finally decided to send a crisis intervention team to help us work out our issues. We had weekly visits from a therapy team for three months. Within the first few weeks with my husband's quiet, compliant demeanor, he had won them over. I was typically very quiet, but now words were spewing nonstop since I had no one to talk to, no support of any kind and was racked with physical and emotional exhaustion. I was extremely overwhelmed and I'm sure I came across as a basket case. I heard a lot of blame being placed on my past from the team and from my husband. This sealed my fate; they couldn't see beyond my label, either. "Foster Child." Was this going to follow me forever?

The crisis intervention team that DFCS sent was not trained in Reactive Attachment Disorder and did not realize that the child they were seeing was not the child that I got once they left. To them, she was loving, sweet and beautiful. They didn't see the behavior I saw because they only saw her in our controlled environment. By now the children knew the rules and were more compliant. We were in the room with them, so Ellen did not do her typical behaviors that she does when you leave the room. They didn't see the real child; they only saw a facade -- but they didn't know that. If they had been trained in Reactive Attachment Disorder, they would have known this from day one. There were so many signs of this disorder that it would have been impossible for them to have missed it . . . had they been trained! For parents unprepared for this disorder, it can be devastating to a family, if they are not educated in advance. If they are educated in advance, it could become a very different and positive experience. A crisis intervention team, working with foster children, untrained in RAD.......hummm.

We had two more visits when one therapist decided to go to school to visit Ellen in a different environment. I was thinking, "Finally! They are finally willing to go into Ellen's environment and see how she is outside of her controlled environment." We sat Ellen down and explained that Ms. Lynne would come to school the following week and play with her and her school mates. Ellen was beyond excited. I was beyond excited!!! I thought, "Finally! They are going to see what I am talking about." I knew that as soon as the therapist went to Ellen's school and she was the center of attention, she would be so over-the-top excited that it would allow the therapist to see the real child who lies beneath. I knew Ellen would not be able to handle the excitement of being #1 and keep her mask up at the same time. I knew that this moment was going to be a revelation to this team. I knew that this moment would be a defining moment in my life, in *our* life. Finally, they were going to see what I deal with each and every day.

171

Two weeks later when our therapy team finally came out for our last family visit, what Ms. Lynne had to say was an eye opener to the team. Ms. Lynne explained that she was surprised and taken aback at what she had witnessed. Indeed, this beautiful, sweet, affectionate little girl morphed before her very eyes into a child she did not recognize. She said Ellen was so excited about her visit that she was running around completely and totally out of control. When Ms. Lynne started to gather the children for group play with Ellen, Ellen started being extremely bossy telling her who would be playing and who would not, what they would be doing and how everyone would play. During the play session, she was completely over the top and out of control. One therapist said, "Little girls often flutter. She was probably just fluttering." Ms. Lynne assured her this was definitely NOT fluttering, and you could tell by the look on her face that she realized she had just wasted three months' worth of therapy. It seemed as if she finally understood what I had been saying all along. It is possible for a child to act totally and completely different in a controlled environment than in a non-controlled environment. Ellen's teacher had already made it clear to Ellen that she was the one in control; however, Ms. Lynne had yet to establish herself as the one in control and this session took a turn for the worse. I might have been the damaged party, but I had done my research and my homework and was doing what I felt was in the best interest of my child. And I think I had just proven my case. This event proved that the structures and controls implemented in my home and on my children were having a profound positive impact on my children.

I feel that, because I was able to control Ellen's extreme controlling behavior with behavior modification techniques instead of medicating her, I was successful in achieving goals that were in her best interest. The Reactive Attachment Disorder books I read all had a few things in common. The care giver needs *a lot* of support, and some of the actions of the care giver may seem abusive to others. They stated that the number one goal of the child was to divide and conquer, often pitting each against the other. It also said that, if the child was able to conquer one parent, it was likely to produce a divided home and often times a broken home. The former was achieved in our home.

In a last ditch effort, I called a therapist in our city who worked with Reactive Attachment children and who was on the list that our Crisis Intervention team left us. A visit for our family was scheduled, and we started going for weekly visits. One week she would work with Ellen and John, and another week she would work with Ellen and me. By now our entire life was wrapped around Ellen, and the boys were typically gated in their playroom. With the boys together without constant supervision, someone was constantly getting hurt and crying; but I had all I could handle with Ellen's school work, therapy work and keeping her occupied. In addition, I still had housework, laundry, outside work and meals to do, as well. John continued to travel but not as much. I was exhausted, depressed and at the end of my rope.

We were attending a mega church at the time, but it was such a big church that I never felt welcomed. It was merely a mad rush in and a mad rush out trying to be one of the first ones in the mass exodus from the parking lot. I felt lost, alone, unlovable and damaged. I wanted to run away from it all. I needed to be in a church where I felt my Father. I desperately needed to feel Him and I couldn't. I often watched Joel Osteen on television and his positive words often helped me make it through another day. I would sit at the television, close my eyes and melt into his words. I would tell myself, "I am a good person, I am loving, I am kind, and I can do this…. I am a good person." I would watch his wife Victoria and listen to her words of admiration for her husband, and I would cry because I wanted to feel that way about my husband again. I needed so badly to feel it and was fearful that I would never get back there. Once again, I couldn't feel anything at all. I had become a robot just doing what I had to, merely to get by.

John and I were finally able to sit down with Ellen's therapist and find out what she had gathered from our visits with Ellen. Her reports diagnosed Ellen with Reactive Attachment Disorder, Chronic Post Traumatic Stress Disorder, as well as a couple of other diagnoses. It was noted that "Ellen has a desperate need for attention and struggles to share with siblings or peers. Ellen has a pervasive desire to control events and people in her life. Ellen needs a family where she is able to enter as an 'emotional infant' that requires intensive emotional attention." She also noted that Ellen's primary need is to build a secure attachment with caring parents. "She needs to continue an open relationship with her brothers, but her emotional health is contingent on building a relationship with *key attachment adult figures. Placement as a sibling unit may place Ellen at risk for another disrupted placement.*"

Ellen's actions and behaviors were not a deal breaker. Ellen's behaviors were not to be feared, but embraced. I believe Ellen was in survival mode and she was merely living life as she had learned it. Her actions were not her fault, but our fault. She was a two year old child when she entered into foster care due to neglect. I truly feel her 7+ placements were the main cause of these behaviors. Did she have the foundation for these behaviors before entering into foster care? Absolutely. She drank from a dog's bowl for water in order to survive. However, instead of us helping her overcome the trauma she suffered before care, we (collectively) ignored it and then added layers and layers to it. Only years later, when she became a "behavior problem," did we start trying to help her overcome her issues. Babies suffer just as much as older children, if not more! I often hear children are resilient. Yes, I think children are resilient under normal circumstances. Ordinary children in consistent families with little or no trauma are resilient, but not our children. We need to start helping our children the day they come into care, regardless of age, not wait until they become a behavior problem. By then it's too late, the damage has already been done. Intensive training on RAD, Post Traumatic Stress Disorder and other common issues with foster children, such as FAS (fetal alcohol syndrome) should be required of every person working with foster children. In addition, foster parents should be trained on *how* to parent the foster child. Currently, it is assumed they are parented pretty much the same as biological children. I can assure you, that is not the case. Should this deter us from fostering, or adopting them? Absolutely not! As long as you are prepared, realistic and committed, it's no harder than parenting biological children. However, it's even more rewarding! To hold a wounded child in your heart and teach them to soar is the greatest reward one can achieve.

Three weeks after getting this report, Ellen brought home a new picture she had drawn in school; and I asked Ellen to tell me about her picture. I was concerned because this was the second disturbing picture Ellen had drawn. The first one was of John and I lying in our bed and Ellen was in our room standing beside me. There was a dagger in her hand and one in mine; there was blood on both Ellen and me. This new picture was even more disturbing. This picture was of the sibling group and made it clear that keeping the siblings together could be a dangerous situation for them. I immediately scanned the picture and emailed it to DFCS. Further, I decided that that was *it* and wrote a letter to DFCS asking them to remove her from my home ASAP. I finally had the proof necessary to prove that keeping the sibling group intact was not the best decision in this particular case.

I knew I had no other choice but to risk losing all three of these children. I truly loved this little girl but was unable to parent her with John and I on different pages; and I was not going to allow her to control my home, my life, or my relationship with my husband. Had we been on the same page with parenting Ellen, this might have ended very differently.

Father's Day weekend, 2009, Ellen went to live with the foster mother who had wanted to adopt her. She would be in a family with one other female biological child who was older than her. Ellen would be the baby in the family, a position in which RAD children typically fair better. The family lived close enough that we could maintain visitation between the children. If I had listened to the foster mother when we began our adoption journey, this fiasco could have been avoided. However, I put my faith in others who worked with Ellen and I judged the foster mother without considering her mothering instincts. She already knew and stated previously that keeping the sibling group in tact was not the best decision for Ellen. She was Ellen's mother and she knew what was best for her. After reading the paperwork, I felt her comment was based on her desire to adopt Ellen without her brothers. But she truly knew what was best for Ellen; after all, she *was* her mother and was in this for all of the right reasons. Ellen has since been adopted by this wonderful family. Before Ellen left, we sat our toddler boys down and explained to them that Ellen would be leaving and explained why in terms that toddler boys could understand.

The weekend Ellen left, I had planned a much needed trip to visit my daughter, Tanya, in St. Petersburg, Florida. I hadn't planned it that way; it just happened to land on the same weekend. When Ellen left, John said he was surprised that she didn't cry, I knew there would be no tears. She was numb inside, just like I had been, just like RAD children, or PTSD children are.

This trip was my first trip away from the kids since the day they walked into our home. I was emotionally, mentally and physically exhausted. I had just spent 10 months fighting desperately to convenience DFCS, a therapy team, my husband's family and my own husband that I wasn't reacting because I was a foster child but that I was reacting because I had three children who were in desperate need of medical intervention. I knew this because I was a foster child and I had seen some of these behaviors before, not because I was allowing my past to distort my view of our children or that I was damaged and mentally unhealthy. Because I had lived what they were living and I knew firsthand how damaging and how traumatic being a foster child truly is, I knew the deep dark emptiness that lived within their hearts and minds, even as little babies.

I personally feel that everyone who works with foster children should be intensely educated on Reactive Attachment Disorder and Post Traumatic Stress Disorder. I truly feel that every foster parent, or foster adoptive parent, and adoptive parent should be intensely trained in these disorders as well. I am telling you, America, you **DO NOT** take children from their known environments without there being severe traumatic effects from it. Maybe if we trained everyone working with foster children on these disorders and parenting children with these disorders, maybe….just maybe, the number of disrupted placements and disrupted adoptions will *finally* start declining. Maybe then, babies like mine will not suffer for years before someone *finally* steps up to the plate to address the trauma they are experiencing every day! Maybe then we can increase the number of children aging out of foster care **SUCCESSFULLY!** Because it's pretty obvious that what we have been doing in the past isn't working. Maybe we should start LISTENING to prior foster children instead of labeling them and ignoring them. I am telling you, foster life is so traumatic, so horrific, that you cannot begin to understand it *if you haven't lived it!*

Chapter 19

To see, feel and touch love again. It felt so good to see someone who loved me and believed in me. It felt so good to hold love in my arms and share a smile that said I'm glad you're mine. I soaked up this wonderful feeling all weekend and spent as much time as I could with this amazing daughter of mine. I didn't want to go home, to face the cold environment that had consumed my home -- but I had to. I had to put my trust in God. I knew He had brought me here. Although there was a lot I didn't understand, I had to give him the reigns and let Him guide me. I had to have faith, although I must add that I had serious doubts.

I relished in that weekend with my daughter. We went sightseeing, walked on the beach, ate lunch on the pier and just enjoyed spending time with each other. We had an incredible weekend together. It felt awesome to have someone care enough about me to want to tend to me for a little while. Tanya made mani and pedi appointments for us, and we spent one of our days being pampered. Tanya knew some of what I was going through, and she knew I needed a little bit of tender love and care. We talked often of the issues I was facing with the children. She was always there for me and was extremely supportive. Although I talked a lot with her, I also shielded her from a lot because I didn't want to put her in the middle of John and I or cause any discord between her and her new siblings. So I had to be careful with what I shared with her. But she knew enough to know what I needed, and I desperately needed this break.

Tanya and I hated for our weekend to come to an end; it seemed as if it ended as quickly as it began. We hated to say goodbye, but life goes on regardless of how we feel. She took me to the airport and we shared a tearful goodbye.

I didn't realize how badly I truly needed this break. I kept thinking, "Why didn't I do this sooner?" I guess I was so caught up in the whirlwind of this little family that I forgot about taking care of myself. I was so overwhelmed that I forgot about me. Before the kids, I worked out several times a week and made sure I indulged in at-home facials, had my nails done biweekly and took time for myself. Now with the kids, all of that was out the window and I no longer existed at all. I no longer existed in my home or in my body. A monster came into my home and ate up everything that made Helen, Helen. I vowed to myself right there and then that I was going to find Helen again and this time I would never let anything make her disappear again.

With Ellen gone, I was *finally* able to focus on Andrew's needs. Billy's needs were primarily medical, besides your typical toddler needs. He was still very docile and easy going even when he was sick. Andrew was very different. When Andrew came to us, he lived in a very dark, sad little world. He was highly emotional and reactive. He was afraid of women and would hit at me any time I came near him. After living with us for about 2 months, he no longer cried for food and was content with waiting until it was prepared. He had gorged on all foods when he came to live with us, but now he only gorged on foods he liked and was becoming selective based on textures and the way he visualized food. After about 4 months, Andrew no longer had toddler diarrhea, was gaining weight and had great skin coloring.

It often seemed as if he lived in his own world. After Ellen left, I immediately involved Andrew in sports. Andrew had issues with different social environments so I made sure I was constantly mixing them up. Andrew often seemed under stimulated and sought constant stimulation; but once he was stimulated, he was easily over stimulated. Then, if you said anything even slightly negative to him, he would immediately wall up and shut down in a depressive state. Trying to keep Andrew balanced was extremely hard. This wonderful little boy desperately needed further investigation.

DFCS finally allowed me to have the boys tested, and we scheduled them both to be seen at the Marcus Institute. At the Marcus Institute, they separated the boys; and they were given many evaluations and tests throughout the day. In the end, it was found that Andrew and Billy both suffered from Fetal Alcohol Syndrome (FAS). Andrew had a more severe case of FAS than Billy, and he also suffered from other complications from FAS. Andrew tested slightly above mental retardation and had other unknown learning disorders. We were given a recommendation to have Andrew tested for special needs PreK, a list of occupational therapists in our area and a list of other resources available for him. Although Andrew tested slightly above mental retardation, I truly felt part of this was due to the neglect he suffered while in care.

Although Billy tested average on his tests, he was diagnosed with an unknown medical condition due to his many health issues. Billy was born three months premature and had Respiratory Syncytial Virus (RSV) as a newborn. He spent many weeks in the hospital and was released to a foster family. When we got Billy he was fairly compliant, very happy and easy going. He was sick almost the entire first two years we had him, but that was all. Billy often suffered from severe asthma attacks, and I spent many nights rocking and loosening mucous in his chest so he could breathe. Billy would be very shaky upon waking every time he went to sleep. It would take him a good 15 minutes before the shakiness went away. We had his blood sugar tested for diabetes, but that came back within normal range. We went through some undiagnosable medical events with Billy, as well. One day he was outside playing. When he started to come back inside, he couldn't move his right leg; it just dragged behind him. Of course we rushed him to Scottish Rite Medical Center, but they couldn't find the cause. This lasted for a couple of weeks and went away as quickly as it came. A few months after that he had a seizure. They think that might have been caused by a fever, but his pediatrician still questioned that because it lacked the stiffness of a typical febrile seizure. He frequently had strange medical events but no one was ever able to piece the puzzle together. It was noted that he had very weak muscle tone and balance issues, all very strange symptoms of something unknown; but his needs seemed to be mainly medical.

What puzzles me is that after hearing Andrew's diagnosis and learning more about FAS, why did it take three years to have it diagnosed? Andrew had almost ALL of the symptoms --low birth weight, small head at birth, low weight gain, diagnosis of failure to thrive, etc. It is noted in his file that his mother tested positive for alcohol and drugs during her pregnancy, so why didn't someone pick up on this before? If he was predisposed to the possibility of FAS, why didn't someone put the pieces together before now? We wasted three precious years when we could have been helping Andrew rewire some of the neurological damage. Instead, we added even more damage to his condition. I would think that anyone working with DFCS and foster children would be required to know all about Fetal Alcohol Syndrome, Reactive Attachment Disorder and Post Traumatic Stress Disorder. Wouldn't that make sense? Read the medical material in a child's file and piece together possible issues to help train the foster parents on the needs of their child/children in order to help the foster child/children overcome instead of adding layers to it. Foster parents are not privy to this medical information; we were because we were in the process of adoption. Only the DFCS team would have had the material and should have had the education to connect the dots. The signs were very obvious. I was dumbfounded. ***Please hear me***; I am not blaming the caseworkers or DFCS, I am blaming the load caseworkers are required to handle due to the lack of government funding. Caseworkers are required to handle caseloads so great that it's impossible to put forth the effort necessary to do justice to their cases, or to their children. Unfortunately, this scenario often creates rapid turnover within the government DFCS system. So now, the child is faced with constant change both in their living environment and the people put in place to make life altering decisions for them. With more budget cuts, the load is even greater and the child is the victim, yet again. Although DFCS is doing the best they can, we cannot continue to sit back and turn our heads. We must all unite and stand up together for change. ***Something*** has GOT to change!

Our children deserve far more than they are currently getting. Do you know how it feels to constantly tell "your story" to individuals over and over again who are supposed to be making important, life changing decisions about you and your future? Our children went through 4 different caseworkers during the two years they were our foster children. That's not enough time to get to know anyone, much less know someone long enough to be making life altering decisions for them.

After we separated Ellen from the sibling group, in order to proceed with the adoption of the boys, DFCS required that I attend 6 months of therapy to show that my past would not be an issue in caring for the boys. I was also required to write a separate letter for both boys to express to them how much I loved and wanted the boys.

I was completely blown away and was thinking, "Did you read the medical reports on these children? They have been in 7 foster homes in 2 years; and I am the only one who cared enough about them to beg, jump up and down like a fool and scream until you guys allowed me to have them evaluated and treatment plans put in place to help them overcome their overwhelming amount of issues. How dare you, once again, point your finger at me?!!" In my eyes, my actions more than showed how much I loved these boys. I loved these boys more than any other mother before me. Their significant overwhelming emotional, mental and physical ailments didn't surface overnight. And when you add in Ellen's enormous amount of issues on top of these, my goodness, even a saint would have broken!

In my eyes, DFCS was not experienced with a prior foster child becoming a foster parent and the immense understanding a prior foster child had that even they lacked. I was keeping my children's best interests at heart no matter what, and I was correct in almost all of my findings. My passion for the rights of these children obviously surpassed what DFCS had become accustomed to from ordinary foster parents. If only every foster parent felt this passionate about their foster children. There are a few who do and I greatly admire them.

DFCS felt that my being a prior foster child was the issue with parenting Ellen and wanted to make sure I would be able to parent the boys without my past causing future problems. They wanted me to attend counseling sessions to be sure I could parent the boys without my past interfering with my ability to parent. That blew my mind. I had two grown children whom I had raised mainly on my own, and they were terrific children. They were very responsible children, both excelled in school, both were college educated and never got into any trouble. I had struggles with Tanya, but nothing extremely serious. However, once I eliminated "family" from the picture, we did wonderfully. Christopher was no trouble whatsoever. Do I have high expectations? Absolutely. When I give a child a directive, I expect for it to be followed the first time I give it and in my timing, not theirs. Does this view of parenting make me a bad parent, or does this type of parenting come from my damaged past? I don't think so.

Once I no longer allowed Ellen unsupervised time with Andrew, he was finally able to have more of a normal life. He even started to allow me to have more of a relationship with him. Andrew was laughing more and allowing himself to enjoy life much more. Although his moods were still extreme, he seemed far less depressed than before. Then after Ellen left, I started seeing a totally different Andrew. I finally had the time to start parenting the boys the way a mother should.

Once again, I'm not saying that everything I put in place for our children when they came to live with us was the right thing to do, nor am I saying that I did everything the right way. However, I do think that from a non-professional's standpoint, I did rather well, especially considering that I had no support, no input, or help of any kind. I feel that, with the medical evaluations, most of the precautions and controls I had in place were indeed validated. When you combine that with the immense stress I was under, I think I did a pretty good job. When Ellen left, she had gone from undereducated for a kindergartener to being ready for 1st grade in 9 months. She couldn't recognize her letters when she came to us and was reading when she left. She was able to give change up to $2.50 and wrote wonderful stories all on her own. She built confidence, was able to play alone in her room for up to 1 hour by herself as long as the door was closed most of the way, and was able to sit in my lap and tell me what she was feeling while rocking. I think I made significant progress, all without medicating her.

After DFCS received my letters, our therapist's evaluation and the testing done by their therapist, it was determined that it would be safe to allow us to adopt the boys. John never had to prove anything. *I* had to prove *myself* because I wore the label, "Foster Child."

But DFCS had done me a favor. Our therapist made me think about myself for a change, I think I was still in a dreamlike state. I say this because, when John and I started dating, I allowed his life to consume mine and I lost me again. My issues with this little family and DFCS forced me to wake up and finally find my voice once and for all. This might seem odd.... but parenting Ellen actually helped me find the biggest part of "me." For the first time ever, I was finally able to answer many of the questions that followed me from my childhood. I was finally able to put closure to so much, and only then was I able to find the empowerment to forge a path to what I feel is God's purpose for my life. I kept asking God why he would bring this little girl into my life only to prove me a failure. However, Ellen is truly the foundation of this enormous passion I feel for the rights of children in foster care. Only because of Ellen have I been able to truly find "Helen." This wonderful, handful of a child is the only reason I no longer have any questions about my past. Ellen helped me close every door that had been open for years, and she has helped me to embrace and love the woman I am today. She lit a fire in me that I can't put out, it burns hotter every day . . . and it feels wonderful. I never thought I could do what I do today until she showed me how to push myself out of my comfort zone. As I was teaching her how to reach beyond her comfort, I was teaching myself at the same time. We were actually learning how to "do life" together! Ellen is my passion and she is my fire. God gave me a wonderful gift: He gave me Ellen....even if for just a little while. I will never be the same because of this wonderful child. For the first time ever, I was able to stand up for myself and I didn't care about trying to keep everyone else happy. I feel free, I feel alive! It feels great...and it was all because of my time with Ellen.

My letters convincing DFCS that I loved Andrew and Billy and truly wanted to be their forever mommy:

My love and desire to keep Andrew

On August 29, 2008 a wonderful little Hispanic boy fell on the porch stairs as his case worker rang our doorbell. As we opened the door, we watched as a very small yet beautiful little boy walk into our home, looked up with dark little teary eyes and smiled. Then, with toddler curiosity, he walked further into our home, into our life and into our hearts.

Andrew is a sweet, yet complicated little fella. Just this morning, I looked at him and wondered what goes on in this little head of his. He is so sweet, his intense ability to love is amazing. How this complicated little boy can emit such unconditional love baffles me. It's a warmth and feeling one would love to cuddle up with each and every day, I love basking in his presence. Yet, below this amazing love lies a very deep complexity, uncharted territory that has yet to be investigated. What could possibly lurk beneath to cause this amazing bundle of love to turn into himself, into such deep dark troubled waters. Waters that roll with such intensity that it washes over him and seemingly pulls his precious little body into a roaring whirlpool of confusion. Uncharted territory, which given time will soon be investigated.

When Andrew came to us, he was a very unhealthy, very depressed and very undisciplined little boy. Andrew would constantly fall to the floor and have tantrums every day, his need for attention was uncontrollable. Andrew was not a little boy I thought I could EVER fall in love with. He hated me, he would swat at me for even looking at him. He would scream at the sight of food and had to have it right away. When he did get food, he would gorge himself. Andrew had toddler diarrhea, failure to thrive and was not digesting any of the food he ate. His growth

185

was stunted and he was the size of an 18 month old. His skin color was clammy and ashen. His eyes were dark, sad, depressed, with not even a hint of light flowing through them. He was sad, never smiled and rarely looked up. The only person who could get any sort of laughter from him was John and only with direct attention. The only person he came to trust in those first few months, was John. I could do NOTHING for him. I couldn't really even get close to him. Andrew lacked an ability to communicate, he had limited vocabulary and often resorted to gesturing and grunting for what he wanted. Andrew was not potty trained and his relationship with his siblings was nothing but chaos and constant fighting. Andrew lived for just one thing every day, what can I do to get most of daddy's attention today, if not all.

Today Andrew is a thriving, small, but adorable 3½ year old. He no longer has tantrums and only pouts some. He has learned patience when it comes to food, he still tends to gorge a little, but something we continue to work on. Andrew no longer has toddler diarrhea or failure to thrive, he has gained weight and has even grown a few inches. Believe it or not, he's a little chunky these days, I call him my chunky monkey at which his eyes sparkle and he laughs. Andrew's need for attention is that of a normal, healthy 3 ½ year old. He can even sit still long enough to watch an entire movie completely through, woohoo. His skin color is gorgeous and his boo boos heal within normal time limits. Andrew has a much larger vocabulary, yet is often garbled and not understandable. Andrew has been able to build a very special, loving bond with his brother Billy. They are finally able to play together with little fighting and chaos. Andrew is also now potty trained, although he does wear a pull up at night.

The biggest change though is in eyes, yes . . . he lights up EVERYDAY . . . . he truly emits a beam of light from his eyes EVERYDAY. (as my eyes get teary writing this) He is so full of joy and happiness. He laughs and smiles all the time, except when he gets into trouble, that's when his beautiful little eyes fill with water. You know what I love the most about him? What I love the most about Andrew these days is his love. When he looks up at me with those beautiful beaming eyes I can fill his heart. I can truly feel the immense love this little boy has for me. It's as if his heart reaches out and hugs me every day. I can truly feel how much this little boy loves me just by looking at me. When he reaches up to hug me, kiss me and pat my face, I just want to melt into his arms. When he looks at me and says, "Mommy, I love you" . . . it takes my breath away. Eight months ago, who in the world would have ever thought this was even remotely possible.

Andrew still has a ways to go academically. Before we can proceed with a plan we must first ascertain what his specific needs are in this area. Andrew has an appointment with the Marcus Institute on June 10. After we receive their evaluation we can then prepare a plan to bring Andrew to where he needs to be developmentally. I feel we have let Andrew down, with Ellen's extensive needs and Billy's medical needs, it has left Andrew's needs on the back burner. He was receiving speech therapy is his past foster home and will need to be placed back into that in the near future as time is freed up for him. Andrew has some learning issues, but with the Marcus Institute evaluation, we will know in what area and how to go about teaching him.

We love this little boy and the thought of losing him rips my heart out. He has come so far and a move could actually cause him possible irreversible damage. Once again, there is something not right about Andrew and change is different for him, he has to take change one small baby step at a time. Even with fun, if it's unfamiliar to him, it has to be done ever so slowly and only then can he handle it. I personally feel a move would cause him to go back into that dark place and this time he may never come out.

I want to be the mom to take him to school on his first day, register him for high school, watch him play ball and meet his future wife. I want to be the new grandmother to cry with him when his first child is born. And, I want him to look at me with those wonderful loving eyes on the day when I must take my very last breath and say good bye to this beautiful world.

My love and desire to keep Billy

On August 29, 2008, a wonderful little Hispanic toddler stood on our porch as his case worker rang our doorbell. As we opened the door, we watched as a very small yet beautiful little boy toddled into our home, looked up with beautiful dark eyes and smiled. Then, with toddler curiosity, he wobbled further into our home, into our life and into our hearts.

Billy is a sweet, adorable, loving little boy with beautiful dark curly hair and the most amazing smile ever put on the face of this earth. When Billy smiles, the whole entire world lights up. This little boy is so full of life and full of energy. He is almost always happy, extremely flexible and just goes with the flow. He was my little bright spot when the world seemed to close in on me. When I was pulled into 15 directions with everyone needing all of me, he would just stand there and smile. Billy was always happy and playful no matter what. He could be feverish, wheezing and unable to breath, yet never cry or ever act like anything was less than wonderful. He is such an amazing little fella.

When Billy came to us, he was a little unhealthy and very small for his age. He would scream at the sight of food and had to have it right away. When he did get food, he would gorge himself. Billy also had some digestive issues which still persist and are monitored with regular doctor visits.

Billy was nonverbal when he came to us, he would gesture and grunt when he wanted something. Billy's biggest issue has been his health. Billy was diagnosed with asthma and has been sick almost the entire time he has been with us. He has been well for approximately 4 weeks now which has been the longest time he has gone without an illness since blessing us with his presence. Illnesses he would pass to me and I would pass back to him. Billy didn't demand a lot of individual attention and was always happy just playing and being a part of whatever was going on. He was a little distant, not wanting to be held for long periods of time. Just a quick hug then down to play, but with over demands in other areas, this was welcomed with open arms. On nights when he would have trouble sleeping, although he never cried for it, I would take him down stairs and rock him to sleep watching as those beautiful little eyes slowly close in blissful sleep.

Today Billy is a thriving, small, but adorable 2½ year old. He has learned patience when it comes to food. He has gained weight and has even grown a few inches. Although Billy has always been happy, now, his happiness exist on a different level and although he has always sparkled, today he shines like a spot light. I didn't realize his happiness could exist on a deeper level until I witnessed it with my own eyes. He is so bubbly, giggly and happy almost all the time. He hardly ever doesn't follow the rules and he's in his terrible two's. He is so easy to love and I do with all of my heart, mind and soul. Billy speaks very well for a 2½ year old now; he even strives for exact pronunciation. Billy is very smart, very inquisitive and wants to learn about everything. He sings all the time, laughs a lot, and is such a pleasure to spend time with. On nights when he can't sleep, he will quietly call out to me and I gladly creep in, pick him up and take him downstairs to fall asleep in his mommy's arms. Billy use to call every woman he saw mommy, but today he knows who his mommy is and you can tell he loves his mommy very much. Billy will even sometimes ask to be picked up and loved on, this being a blessing since I have more time to devote a little attention to him now days. Billy has been able to build a very special, close, loving bond with his brother Andrew. They are finally able to play together with little fighting and chaos.

Billy still has some unknown medical issues which will be investigated in his June 10 appointment with the Markus Institute. Issues which have been placed on the back burner to enable us to deal with Ellen's extensive needs.

We love this little boy and the thought of losing him rips my heart out. Although Billy stills seems to be able to adapt easily to new environments, it's only a matter of time that the scars are unable to heal without leaving damage behind. He's my baby boy and I couldn't imagine life without him.

I want to be the mother to take him to school on his first day, register him for high school, watch him play ball and meet his future wife. I want to be the new grandmother to cry with him when his first child is born. And, I want him to look at me with those big sparkling eyes on the day when I must take my very last breath and say good bye to this beautiful world.

Chapter 20

I love Spring; it's my favorite time of year. To me Spring signifies new birth, new growth, and often times a new start. New flowers are born, they grow, they stretch in the warm sun and they dance in the rain. Animals give birth and their young play and frolic in the newness of beautiful, luscious Spring growth. Spring brings Easter and it's the saddest, yet most miraculous time of year for me. To me, Easter signifies the death of a little girl's heart. The death of a little girl's heart whose childhood was stolen. A little girl so broken and battered that mere words will never exist to convey it. But today, today Easter signifies the start of new life, the start of new beginnings. Spring is the season my Father gave me new life, new beginnings, and a season of healing. This Spring....our two little boys became ours and we started our new life together. This Spring is a new beginning for our new family.

In April of 2010, we were asked to meet at the DFCS office with the boys and sign our adoption papers. We signed the papers and then we celebrated with cake. After our long journey of ups and downs, we were finally at the finish line. These two amazing little boys were finally going to be ours, and no one will ever be able to take them from us.

On June 21, 2010, these two amazing little boys became Ramaglias. We built a swimming pool and had a huge adoption party. Family and friends all came and we had a wonderful time. The boys loved their new names and repeated them over and over. We named Andrew – Andrew John Ramaglia and Billy became William Joseph Ramaglia. John's name is John Joseph Ramaglia so we shared a little piece of him with both of our boys. We had never taught the boys their biological last names, so the change wasn't hard for them once the adoption was final. However, they knew they had a forever mommy and daddy and would never be moving again. We are open with them about their adoption and the plight of the foster child. They pray for the little boys and girls with no mommies and daddies every night.

Today, Andrew is a completely different little boy. It's very natural and common for him to run up to me for a hug just because he wants one. Andrew still struggles in school because of his special needs, but he is such a loving wonderful little boy. In the past few months he's actually started to become more of a momma's boy. He will rub my back and check on me to make sure I'm doing well. He will often come by just to give me a hug or a kiss. He's momma's little helper, anytime I lose anything he is the first one I go to help me find it. This is one of his little OCD tendencies, but one of those good little quirks. It amazes me how different he is. He laughs all the time and loves life. He beams with rays of sunlight and is pure joy to spend time with. He has come a long way and continues to improve every month. Andrew is now able to enter any new social setting and be a part of the group without any hesitation. This little boy who was nonverbal two years before is now using words far advanced for his years. The little boy who once tested slightly above mental retardation, is now testing average in most areas and above average in a couple of areas. He has other issues with his FAS, is considered Special Needs and is on an individual education plan (IEP) in school. However, we have come far with Andrew; and we are extremely proud of the wonderful child he is becoming. We believe he will eventually overcome his special needs and will join the general population in school. But think of how much further he could have been today if we had identified his disorder as early as possible and helped him overcome it instead of adding to it when he entered foster life. Today, Andrew is more than twice his arrival weight and has grown 6 sizes in 2½ years. I continue to research and seek new parenting tools related to his special needs. I am still seeking a therapist close by who handles children like Andrew. It continues to be a struggle to find adequate help for children like Andrew because of the cutbacks imposed on special children with Medicaid benefits. Andrew only gets depressed when he doesn't get something he wants, gets into trouble, or is in an unfamiliar situation where he must struggle, such as homework, etc. This poor little baby who walked through our door as a very sick little boy now has a chance in life. Andrew now has a chance in life because someone believed in him, someone cared about him and someone finally loved him enough to push the envelope hard enough to procure the help and support he was desperately in need of.

The winter prior to their adoption was Billy's best winter ever. It was Billy's first winter without any illnesses and we were tickled. Although Billy remains very tiny for his age, he has grown into a healthy little boy. His muscle tone and balance is where it needs to be for a little boy of his age. He is extremely intelligent and loves to master electronic gadgets. Billy is a normal, typical little boy of his age. He is very well behaved, loves to push his limits -- as it should be for a child his age -- and is a pure pleasure to share life with.

Both boys are very well behaved, and we often get compliments on their behavior when we are in public. The chaos that existed when they came to our house has been tamed, and they now play like children their ages should play. Of course, we still get the "boy" stuff, but they are pretty much typical little boys. For the most part, the boys are now in maintenance mode; and I have been able to relax most of the controls that were put in place when they came to live with us. Although Andrew is allowed to have unsupervised play with Billy, there is a limit to the number of "accidents" allowed. Does this come from my horrific past and my siblings hurting me? Or does it come from a place of love that provides safety for my children? I say it comes from a place of love that provides safety for my children, but I am much more aware of this situation and the damage it can cause to a sibling because of my past. Is that a bad thing, or just a heightened sense of awareness? I say it's a heightened sense of awareness and is a huge positive for me. In fact, I believe this heightened sense of awareness actually makes me a better foster parent/foster adoptive parent -- rather than a risk -- to foster children. I look at these two little boys and am amazed at how far they have come.

The big kids (Tanya, Chris and Tori) visit often, and we all get along very well. We love family game night where we all get together and play Mario or other video games. We spend as much family time together as possible. We try to make sure we do a big kid/little kid vacation in alternating years. Every other year we concentrate on the little kids. I look forward to taking grandkids with us every other year in the future. The more the merrier!

The big kids sometimes babysit so John and I can have a weekend together, to concentrate on "us." We have all come to love, embrace and enjoy our special family. We might not be blood kin, but we share a family bond just as deep. I saw this somewhere on the internet and loved it: "Family isn't always blood. It's the ones in your life who want you in theirs, who accept you for who you are, will do anything to see you smile & LOVE YOU no matter what." We play as a family, enjoy life as a family and we pray as a family.

I am so excited! We found a new church family thanks to my new friend, Carla. I met Carla when the wife of one of John's friends had a Pampered Chef's party. She mentioned wanting to foster and we immediately connected. I gave Carla my phone number, and it was the start of something wonderful.

Carla called me one day and brought her little boy over for a play date. We spoke about foster care and the adoption process for foster children. I was still teaching adoption classes at that time and gave her quite a bit of information. While we were visiting, I told her I was looking for a church and she told me about Alpharetta First United Methodist Church where she and her family attend. It sounded like the type of church family I was looking for, and I had previously heard of this church from a couple of other families in our neighborhood. I told John about it and asked if he would mind if we checked it out.

As we entered the church for the very first time, it felt as if I was "coming home." We got there pretty early, so we were the first people in the sanctuary. As I walked up the aisle, I stopped and took in the beauty of the rich wood surrounding the ceiling. Then I noticed the chandelier; it was very unique. The chandelier was made of the same wood as the ceiling and created a very intricate cross in the center of the room. It was breathtaking. As we sat down, it felt as if my Father walked up behind me and engulfed me in the biggest hug I had ever felt. It was as if He was saying, "You are finally home, my daughter. Welcome to my house, to *our* home." It was as if God was bringing me home to do His work in His house. And I knew from that very first moment that I was home, that I was in God's house and He would take it from there. At that very moment, I felt beyond a shadow of doubt that God has a true purpose in my life and that this would be my home while I complete the task my Father has put before me. I don't know exactly what that is, but I know I'm on the right track and I know He is guiding me. I can feel it.

After people started flooding the pews, a little old lady asked my name. I know I must have had tears in my eyes when I told her. She shook my hand, and then she gave me a big hug and said welcome. John wasn't sold on a new church quite yet, but it was so important to me that I attend this church. After several Sundays, John started to soften a little more; and now he, too, enjoys our church almost as much as I do. I quickly became a member of the Chancel Choir, as did my daughter-in-law, Tori. We were blessed enough to participate in their huge Christmas event, which was so meaningful to me. Here I was finally in my Father's house where I belong with a new church family who seemed to love me no matter what, and I was able to share my favorite time of the year blessing my Father and thanking Him for the wonderful life he has blessed me with. He came to me at Christmastime; and ever since that amazing gift of God's love, Christmastime has taken on a much deeper meaning for me. It is the time of the year when I feel closest to my Father. To be a part of such a beautiful celebration of Jesus' birth was the perfect way to start my "new life."

As John and I started plugging into church activities and volunteer work, we have been able to have a common goal in mind: creating a God-centered marriage and a God-centered family. Today we pray as a family and we study God's Word as a family. We still have a long way to go; but I know we are on the right path and that, in the very near future, my husband will once again see me with the eyes of the man in the silhouette. I have faith in my Father, and I know from experience that His timing is far different from my timing.

All of a sudden in a matter of months, my life was finally coming together and it started taking on new meaning. It seemed as if all of the suffering I had been through was all coming together with a definite mission in mind. I think maybe God needed for me to suffer in order to understand all of the little nuisances of the foster life. Only through the trials of becoming a foster parent and parenting God's special children was I able to understand what *I* was feeling all those years. Only then did I understand that deep dark pit and the beast called "The Unknown." Only through my suffering has a fire been kindled inside of me, burning big and hot. Only now am I equipped with the tools necessary to do my Father's work. Only through this suffering have I come to understood what I feel is God's purpose for my life. Only now do I feel equipped with the intense passion necessary to accomplish that "something important" God needs me to accomplish.

One day at church Carla asked me if I would speak for a foster child organization she was volunteering with. I had never thought much about doing something like this as speaking was not my forte, but I accepted. I spent weeks struggling, preparing and fretting over the thought of speaking in front of people. Would my stuttering come back? Would I freeze up? What was I going to say? How does one take the immense amount of trauma in my life, the countless lessons learned and narrow it down to one 15 minute speech? I met with the Board of this organization, and they offered to help me with my speech. I gave them the pages of my haphazardly written memoir notes, and they found a way to help me put 40 or 50 pages of spewed out words into a 15 minute speech that penetrated hearts, opened minds and educated many. There were many tears shed that night by both women and men; they finally understood a little bit about how traumatic it truly is to be a foster child. What topped off this story was that we ended it with Mom Chase. Mom Chase came from Pooler to read the poem I had written to her many years ago. It was a captivating moment for many. Here, standing in front of them, was a woman who opened her heart and her home to a traumatized little girl whom she didn't know and gave her a soft place to heal. This special woman was standing there reading the words of the traumatized little girl she saved. For the many who were on the verge of tears, this was the breaking point. I don't think there was a dry eye in the building that night.

To my amazement, all the fear I had been feeling for weeks dissolved the moment I stood at that podium. The moment I stood in front of everyone, this quiet, mousy, introverted, little woman suddenly found an amazing calmness. This woman, who was so scared and nervous that she forgot to rinse the conditioner out of her hair, spoke with assertiveness, passion, and pain and was able to articulate traumatic moments with intense passion . . . without breaking down. I had to stop for a few seconds several times to keep my composure, but I knew right then and there what God was leading me to do. As I was speaking, I only wished I could have spoken longer -- there was so much more I suddenly wanted to say. I felt a passion I had never felt before; and I found that when I speak about these children, something happens. I can't explain it, but I know this has something to do with that "important thing" God needs for me to do. I can feel it.

Since that night, I feel different. Something happened inside of me. I found "me." Who would have thought that this mousy, introverted woman would find herself by pushing herself out of her comfort zone? I did for me what I had done for Ellen: I made me get out of my little box and try something scary. Then I understood how she felt. But it made me feel even more secure in my theory about her because I did it myself, and the means definitely justified the end. This moment would define the "me" that I am today. Had I not committed to that speech that day, I might not have realized my passion. I no longer feel that lost feeling anymore. I truly feel this is God's purpose for my life. Advocating for, working with, and educating the public on foster children. There is a fire, a passion in me that burns hotter each and every day for the rights and needs of foster children. Only now do I understand the necessity for this book. It is my hope that this book will help walk in the shoes and feel the heart of the foster child. A person must walk in a foster child's shoes in order to understand how to help them. And even then, they still cannot understand the true impact of being "nobody's child." That does something to a child that's impossible to explain -- the words don't exist!

After speaking, I found I desperately needed to work with foster children so I set out on a course that would open my eyes. In working with many foster child organizations, I found that they were all working with a lot of children who were only plugged into that one resource. There was no collaboration and I kept hearing the word "competition." I found the children were only getting one or two of their needs met and, at the end of the day, had many needs going unmet. How can we create successful foster children if their needs are not being met? How can we meet their many needs, if we are afraid of competition? There is no such thing as competition when we are working with this population of children. It's called collaboration, not competition. . . . *never* competition! So I created a nonprofit organization, Fostering SuperStars (www.fosteringsuperstars.org), where I connect foster children to all of the resources available to them. As I worked with organizations providing support for children in foster care, I found that each organization had different children they were providing services for. I saw the need for one primary organization to work with all of the organizations and see to it that each child received support from all the resources available and to secure additional resources to provide for the *many* unmet needs leftover.

I helped create the materials and process for a mentoring program for foster children, One 4 Life. This is a lifelong mentoring commitment, not just a one or two year commitment. Our children are in need of a lifelong, consistent partner -- a Life Partner. Every child deserves one consistent person in their life, for life. My future goal is to start working on a voucher program and hopefully pull together "One Voice," a program where prior foster children who have aged out and have dedicated their lives to advocating for children in foster care come together as one large voice to educate, inspire and transform tomorrow for today's children in crisis, children in pain, nobody's children, America's forgotten children......children in foster care!

I look at all that I am currently doing on behalf of foster children, at my family and where I am today. How did I get here? It's been 2 years since our adoption and my life has completely changed! How did I get from there to here? I love what God is doing with me, how

He is using me. I feel I am finally home and doing what I am meant to do. How many people in life truly know what this feels like? I am so blessed. I am God's little miracle, and I hope He continues to feel I am worthy of His work.

Chapter 21

Oh, what is that? I do believe I hear a ring at the door . . . .

I remember a little girl sitting in her room watching as her mind played a scene of life to be. Was I merely daydreaming that day, or did God give me a glimpse of the future? The little girl sits back and watches as an amazing woman full of confidence walks down the foyer of a beautiful home . . . her home. The little girl watches as she admires the pair of slacks the woman is wearing and listens to the sound of her matching heels hitting the wooden floor. All of a sudden, the little girl watches as this confident woman opens the door and smiles a beautiful smile. It's the smile of a woman loving life and full of confidence and self-esteem. Could this be, could it truly be that this woman is. . . . Me? I sit here in amazement and I feel so blessed. What have I done so wonderful that my Father feels I am this deserving? Could it be, could it truly be that this is my life? I feel so different, what has happened?

. . . .I open the door and in front of me is my wonderful son and his wife. Christopher finished college and is married now. He and his wife have just purchased their first house and are in the process of slowly making it theirs. Christopher has just started his first big job since college as a systems engineer for a health care company here in Alpharetta. We get together often and enjoy the time we spend together. Christopher and I often have mother/son days when we get together and have lunch and go shopping or some other activity, even if it's just hanging out and talking. Tori, Chris' wife, and I often do pampering things together, as well. We are hoping to start an every-other-Sunday deal where they come to church with us, and we spend family Sunday together.

Tanya has since moved to Alpharetta and works as a surgical assistant to a doctor who works in the ophthalmology field. She has come a long way. She put herself through college while working full time and is seriously considering her masters in occupational therapy. We have carved out a very special and close mother-daughter relationship. I look at her and I can see me. She knows I love her unconditionally and that feels really, really good. She knows I'll give my advice if she asks for it but will stand behind anything she decides without judging her, knowing she has to make her own mistakes in life.

Mom and I have carved out a unique relationship between the two of us, also. Mom and I started talking about the events and issues that surrounded Ellen and our little family. Once Ellen left and I was able to calm down enough to understand what I was truly feeling, for the first time ever, I was able to call Mom and talk about what was going on in my life. For the first time ever I was able to allow Mom to be a mother to me. I was able to feel for the first time ever that I wasn't putting her in the middle of anything while I was sharing my side, but that I was allowing her to mother me. I have come to find that's what mothers do -- they listen without feeling as if they are being put in the middle. All those years I thought I was protecting her by not sharing the intimate details of my life, she thought I didn't trust her enough to share my life with her. On her Mother's Day card last year I thanked her for being my mother all those years even though I didn't allow her to take that role in my life. I could never understand why then, but now I understand and am finally able to be a daughter to her for the first time ever.

Mom recently had her kidney removed, and I went to the hospital to stay the night with her. It was her first night out of surgery and she was in a lot of pain. She felt bad the next day that she had kept me up most of the night, but I thanked her for the opportunity to know what it felt like to be there for my mom when she needed me the most. I explained that for years I would hear other women talk about the stuff they did with their moms or things they were doing for their moms now that they were older and needed to be taken care of. I never thought I would have the opportunity to know what that felt like, but she gave me the opportunity to know what it felt like to truly be a daughter. I thanked her for that opportunity. As I left, there were tears in our eyes; and for the first time ever, I could feel her heart. It was the heart of a mother. I had a mother all those years . . . why couldn't I find her? Was I so deep in that dark pit that I couldn't find my way to her? When I got down to my car, I just sat and cried. I finally knew what it felt like to be a daughter. Was I too scared to allow myself to find her before now? This beaten and battered little girl finally knew what it felt like to have a true mother-daughter moment. God has given me so many gifts this year. I looked up at my Father and I asked him what have I done so wonderful that I have deserved this many gifts lately. And then I laughed at the words that where coming out of my mouth. Is this truly my life? I'm not used to this, but I could definitely get used to it very quickly.

John and I have come a long way. We continue to build our marriage; but to be honest, I think that because of all we have been through, we will actually be able to build a much better marriage than we could have had if we had not taken this journey. We both have a lot to overcome, including John. Only through fighting for my children did I find my voice and the strength to fight for something I felt passionate about. Only through this struggle did I find the strength to stand up for myself and not defer to someone else's wants or desires. Only through this struggle was I finally able to find "me," and only now am I able to give "me" to him. I feel the future is very promising, and I look forward to the fruits of our struggles. God has a plan for us and the best is yet to come. We continue to see Brenda, our therapist, and will continue for a very long time to come. She has helped us understand a lot about ourselves, about our marriage and about each other. I can feel John ever so slowly opening his heart to me these days. We just celebrated our 5th wedding anniversary in Helen, Georgia. It was the perfect ending to the perfect year for me. It reminded me of my other family with whom I was able to share some time during this past summer.

After 35 years, our Emmanuel Baptist Church of Kerkrade group had its first reunion ever this past summer . . . and it was wonderful. For the first time since I left Holland in 1980, I got to see many of the faces of the dear people who helped create the foundation of who I am today. At the reunion, we were supposed to stand up and tell everyone what our years at that church meant to us. I had the opportunity to stand up and tell this wonderful group of people how truly important they were to me. It was very emotional and tears were shed. It felt amazing to tell these unknowing people the role they had played in creating who I am today. In closing, I urged them to read my website, so they could understand the true impact they had made on a child's life. When they came in the next morning, there were even more tears as they read the story of my suffering and finally understood the critical role God had allowed them to play in the creation of "me." At the exact time the United States was severing my father's parental rights and giving its permission for me to move abroad with my foster family, a group of five people were starting a church that would play a vital role in who I have become.

My phone rang the other night, and Dad Chase was rushed to the hospital. I quickly packed and went to Savannah. It was my turn to stay the night at the hospital with him. I watched this wonderful, fragile man lay in bed struggling for every breath he took. I watched while embracing the quiet of the night and memories of another time, another place where this amazing man was a young, healthy soldier and a father to a child no one else wanted. This man whom I adored was now lying in a hospital bed struggling for every breath. To our amazement, God chose to give him more time with us on this precious earth. I cherish every minute I get to spend with this amazing father of mine. Although Dad has a hard time hearing me, especially on the phone, he called just to thank me for coming, for spending time with him at the hospital. I know one day I will have to say goodbye to this wonderful father of mine, but I know he loves me. . . . . . .he told me so on my wedding day, at the hospital, and again today on the telephone. And I believe him -- his actions say he truly loves me. I know beyond a shadow of doubt that I have a father on this earth, and that he truly does love me. Next week, I am taking a copy of this manuscript so he can read it. I want to be sure he knows how important he is to me, was to my life and the woman I have become. Before God takes this wonderful man home, he will have read this book; and I will be forever blessed because of it, because he will finally know how truly special he is too me and how much I truly love him.

Mom and Dad Chase, you have truly been a blessing to me and to my life. I am who I am today, because you opened your hearts and your home to a traumatized child who was lost, alone, unwanted and completely broken. It has been a long, hard road for all of us, but today we are a family. We have each other and we love each other very much. We are finally here, and that's all that matters! I love you both very much. Thank you for your patience. Thank you so much for being there 38 years later when I finally allowed you to love me, to finally take your place as my Mom and Dad. I've said those words for years, but today they ring sweet in my heart. I can finally feel it in my heart. Thank you so much for allowing me the opportunity to truly be a daughter. I love you both so very much!

I am Helen, I am a prior foster child, I am a mother and a wife, I am a foster adoptive mother, I am the founder of Fostering SuperStars, I am a volunteer with One 4 Life and KidS[3], I am a child of God and a *very* strong advocate for foster children. I am a strong woman, full of confidence and ready to fight the fight of my life. . . . . . .I am ready to fight just as hard for my 500,000 other children who live in foster care, who are muddling through life every day in a traumatized shell of a body, as I did for the two who now bear my name. I cannot adopt them all, but they are all mine -- and I will fight the fight of my life for them.

America, it's time for us to accept our responsibility and educate ourselves on this ever growing crisis. If we open our arms today, we will start a movement where foster children no longer fear the label "foster child" because it will no longer carry the stigma it carries today. If we start correcting this problem as a community, then there will be a tomorrow where there is no crisis. If we educate our children today, they will not fear a child, who is different, but will embrace the child in kindness and help fill the many voids that exist in the lives of foster children.

With the state of our economy, foster care is in crisis. Children are dying, both in and out of foster care. I don't know if we will ever be able to fix "the system," but I'm not worried about "the system." I'm worried about "the child." If we band together so children in foster care have the same experiences as children in biological families, then it really doesn't matter how the system is doing. If we make sure "our children" are thriving, are learning, are healthy and whole -- just like all of our other children, it doesn't matter what the government does. "Our children" will not be in distress because *we* have parented them to the ***best of our ability***.

It truly takes a village to raise a foster child; one set of foster parents cannot provide everything a foster child needs. It takes an entire community of individuals pitching in and doing everything they can to see to it that the children in foster care in their community are getting ALL of their needs met. If there are gaps, they need to step up to the plate and find a way to secure the resources to meet those needs. Not necessarily money....RESOURCES, such as dentists, ophthalmologists, beauty parlors, bakeries, clothing retailers, shoe retailers, sports equipment retailers, photographers, tutoring providers, extra circular activity providers, therapist, and the list goes on and on. Not everyone can be a foster parent, but everyone can do something for a foster child . . . and should. Let's get in the schools and educate our children; let's talk about it. When you ignore it, it makes the child in foster care feel different, feel dirty. It's time for us to step in and get our hands dirty, America! I promise you, after you do, it's going to change your heart. Our children are hurting and they don't want to hurt anymore. All they want is to feel loved.... truly loved, wanted and valued.

Just think, if every adult Sunday School class in America were to sponsor a foster child, we could create that small community of care each child needs. If they follow that child through life, if that child has a Life Partner as well, and all of their needs are met by community resources, we would be parenting that child (our child) to the best of our abilities. If we all work together in a collaborative effort, this could be done . . . and *should* be done, for the sake of our children!

Help me help precious little children who cannot help themselves. Let's love them unconditionally; let's not judge them. They are worthy and they are so very precious. Are they hard to parent? Yes, they are. It's not going to be easy; but in time....with education and *consistent*, firm, loving discipline . . . they, too, will come to trust again and then to love again. They must first feel loved, truly loved in order to give love back. How can you give something you know nothing about? Let's teach them what love is, let's **show** them what unconditional love truly is.

God commands us to care for the orphans and widows in distress. I truly feel that God has put this burden on my heart and on my shoulders, and I love my Father enough to do what He has commanded me to do. There is something important He needs for me to do ...... and I am His.

Come.... walk with me.

Nobody's Child

Who is "Nobody's Child" today? Let me introduce you to a very few:

As I write this, there is an autistic foster child about to graduate high school. He is extremely smart but is unable to navigate the journey into college by himself and needs an advocate to guide him, to partner with him. However, because one person has not committed themselves to helping this young man who desperately wants to attend college, he won't be going. Instead, this bright young man will probably go into an institution because there is no one to care for him after he ages out of the system. I find this heartbreaking. And this is only one of many, many stories like this.

When we made two telephone calls to obtain authorization for three children who had requested mentoring partnerships, we were asked if we could mentor the other 100+ children in their care, as well. Two telephone calls in one county, and we cannot even begin to provide the number of requested mentors. There are just not enough Life Partners/Mentors, or organizations designed to mentor foster children, to fill this monumental need.

There is a foster child with cancer who is suffering through his third round of chemotherapy by himself, alone, feeling hopeless and helpless. He is just one of many cases of foster children suffering through catastrophic illnesses alone, by themselves.

We took a foster child home from camp; and when we drove up, we found what belongings he was allowed to keep, packed in black garbage bags sitting on the sidewalk. He had just told us he had

had the best week of his life, that he finally felt wanted, valued and loved, and that he was ready to be a better child. In the blink of an eye, everything changed. He was devastated, crying and begging to stay. He was immediately carted away, back into the world of "the unknown"....alone. We have no idea what has become of him -- we lost track of him that day. This story is not unique, this happens numerous times....EVERYDAY!!!

Do you know that most foster children who "age out" of foster care are lacking the skills necessary to become successful adults?

Do you know that most of these children will become homeless after leaving foster care or be arrested or, worse yet, be sold into the sex trade industry?

Do you know that most children who "age out" of foster care will not have a driver's license, a car, a way to afford car insurance, reliable references nor transportation to acquire a job?

Do you know that once a foster child ages out of care, we have no way to track where they go or what happens to them?

After a foster child turns 18, or sometimes 21, America is no longer liable for this child and they no longer matter. They are....

....Nobody's Child

The Ramaglia Family 2012

**John, Helen, Tanya, Tori, Christopher
Andrew, Billy**

Fostering SuperStars

What does Fostering SuperStars do?

As I worked with organizations providing support for children in foster care, I found that each organization had different children they were providing services for. I saw the need for one primary organization to work with all of the organizations and see to it that each child received support from all the resources available and to secure additional resources to provide for the *many* unmet needs leftover. Thus, began Fostering SuperStars. **Our focus** is "the child," to address the needs of every foster child by plugging them into resources already available to them and then finding resources in the community to fill the many voids. By matching each foster child with a life partner (a lifelong mentor), through a partner organization, and having their life partner inventory the many needs that still need to be met, we can finally meet EVERY need our children have. With our child's inventory list in hand, we go out into the community to find businesses and individuals willing to fill the needs where there are no resources yet available. This will allow every foster child to receive "complete wrap-around support." If we want to create "successful" foster children, we must meet ALL of their needs, not just some of their needs. Through this collaborative effort, we actually add a layer of protection and accountability where this child and his/or her life and future is concerned.

Our goal is to connect each and every child in foster care with organizations, partnerships and providers to meet the numerous unmet needs these children have. Our goal is to meet 100% of their needs, not just a few. **Only then** will successful foster children become the norm and not the exception.

We accomplish this goal by:

Recruiting Mentors, CASA workers, Foster Parents and Foster Adoptive Parents by raising awareness and support for foster children in our communities. Every child deserves a Life Partner to "do life" with, someone who will be there throughout their lives, not just for a year or two.

Raising public awareness so foster children will no longer feel the emotional burden of rejection. Every child just wants to be loved and accepted for who they are no matter what their life circumstances are.

Recruiting successful prior foster children to join our "One Voice" initiative for foster children. Our hope is to bring together former foster children who have turned their lives around and are paying it forward by advocating for foster children. Yes, singularly we can make changes; but when we come together as one....we can create miracles.

Being raised as a foster child myself, turning my world from foster to fabulous on my own, and now becoming a foster adoptive parent as well, gives me a perspective most people never see or experience. It's a full circle accomplishment in the foster world. This gives me the unique ability to raise public awareness for foster children and the needs of these children by sharing my personal experiences through speaking engagements and charity benefits.

Foster children are America's forgotten children, and it's time we reach out and give these children an opportunity to succeed. If I can take a horror-filled childhood and turn it into a fabulous life, these children can do it as well. It is crucial that we develop and provide the support structure necessary to ensure the success of these children.

Although we have several organizations we work with, we don't have nearly enough. We are in desperate need for more foster mentoring organizations. This is where our work begins. It is crucial that we have people willing to step up and mentor our foster youth -- not a one or two year commitment, but a lifelong commitment. For many of our children, this will be as close as they ever get to family. Every child deserves one consistent person in their life, for life. Every child deserves a Life Partner . . . What about YOU?

_____

www.fosteringsuperstars.org

To Potential Foster Parents
and Potential Foster Adoptive Parents

I know the story you have just read is a lot to absorb. For those who are considering fostering, or foster adoption....Yes, it's hard; but I promise you, it's also the most rewarding thing you will ever do in your life! Honestly, if you arm yourself with the necessary tools, you can help create a miracle. You truly can. *You*....can truly change a life.

Our children are so precious and it's unfortunate some must live traumatic lives. However, you can be the one to show a child how to love again. You can teach a child how to trust again. They are merely children who want nothing more than to be loved. You MUST be patient with them and allow them to heal in their own timing. They will probably push you away at first, and they might even sabotage every effort put forth. However, if you show them that you will stand by them no matter what, in time......slowly, they will come to trust again. And their love...will be unlike anything you have ever known before.

Please open your hearts and open your homes to life's most amazing children, our foster children, America's forgotten children. Every child deserves a family! Will you be that family?

Below are the web page addresses of some amazing people who have done just that. They have opened their hearts and their homes to some amazing children and they have created informative, inspirational web pages to share their journey and offer a plethora of information on foster children. They offer support unlike anything I have ever seen before. As experienced as I am, I often find myself surfing their sites for ideas, answers, inspiration or just a pat on the back when I'm in need. I also follow them on Twitter and on Facebook.

Adoptive Legacy   adoptivelegacy.com/

Foster Adoption   fosteradoptionblog.wordpress.com/

Foster 2 Forever   foster2forever.com/

While in the publishing process, I learned that a book was published that bore a title close to mine. As I did further investigation, I found Capri lived in the same city as me, has the very same birthday and a dog just like mine. Not only does this book bear a title close to mine, it is almost like a continuation of my book. My story is the heart, soul and inspiration of the foster journey and her book is the instrument to teach foster children "how" to turn their lives around.

Capri and I have since met for dinner and have plans to further our causes together, as well as individually. After all, it *is* all about collaboration, not competition.

"From Foster Care to Fabulous - An Imperative Movement" – By Capri Cruz

*There are many other sites from foster parents, foster adoptive parents and former foster youth as well.

Dedication

This book is dedicated to the memory of my biological mother, Diana Gay Charbonneau Hall; to the memory of my stand-in mother, my oldest sister, Dorothy Hall Shumpert; and to the memory of my step-mother, My Mommy, Glenda.

This book is dedicated to my former foster parents, John Chase and Shirley Chase Rose. Thank you for opening your hearts and your doors to a child in crisis and giving her a soft place to heal.

To my biological children, Tanya and Christopher, thank you for taking this journey with me, for loving me unconditionally and for growing up with me.

To my husband, John and our two foster adopted boys, thank you for making my life complete. I look forward to the rest of our lives, together.

To Gail, you have been with me through so much. Thank you for my Christmas gift (the job) and for taking a chance on me. Thank you so much for doing the first edits on my book; I truly could not have done this without you!

To Bill, thank you for teaching me about God when I lived in Holland and for helping to mold the woman I have become. Thank you for reading my haphazardly written manuscript and helping me form the story it is today.

…. And to all the foster children in the world today, you are beautiful, you are fabulous, and you can be anything you want to be -- if you want it bad enough. Reach for the stars, and don't let go!!!!

Emmanuel Baptist Church Reunion July 2011

Tanya, Helen & Christopher
December 9, 2006

CPSIA information can be obtained at www.ICGtesting.com
Printed in the USA
LVOW041046150912

298843LV00002B/4/P